Forward

The Irish Wolfhound is not the easiest of breeds having more foibles than most. Consequently, there is an enormous amount of work, which goes into breeding.

At Bonaforte we are keen to follow through with health issues, considering ourselves very lucky to have Dr Serena Brownlie, one of the best Veterinary Cardiologists of all time, looking after the heart health of our hounds.

As owners, you can play an enormous role in helping to improve the health of the breed with your input and feedback. Without you, and the joy I see my hounds bring you, I would have stopped breeding long ago. I just want to say a huge thank you to all of you who bring your Irish Wolfhound back for heart testing and keeping us informed about any health matters. It has helped us develop the Kennel's health and the decisions that we make for the future.

I would like to offer special thanks and sincere appreciation to Ali Irvine who tirelessly helped with both practical and written work (especially the chapters about grooming and Amichien Bonding), Amanda Brown for her Puppy Diary with Rupert, special thanks to Maggie Holder, who shares experiences and knowledge. To Hugh Broadbent, husband, and photographer, thank you. Last to the Oelmühle Kennel for their kindness and generosity.

I hope you find the guide interesting, recognising your contributions in my long-term mission to never stop learning and discovering the intricacies of breeding and rearing Irish Wolfhounds. All breeders no matter how hard they try will eventually produce a defect, that's just breeding. The problem occurs when they don't do anything about it, but hopefully, together we can keep the breed fit and healthy.

There is a degree of repetition in the guide, which is deliberate I assure you: Some of the items are so important, that reiterating them helps reinforce the notion and hopefully helps any reader recall them.

I wish you every joy in the world with your puppy; they are a beautiful breed with soulful Irish eyes.

Carla du Rose

Bonaforte Irish Wolfhounds
www.bonaforte.com

CHAPTER 1

Welcome to the Irish Wolfhound Owners Puppy Guide

While being the proud owner of an Irish Wolfhound puppy is a huge delight it also brings with it a tremendous responsibility. You are instantly in charge of rearing a giant breed puppy into fully developed adulthood. This guide gives you an insight as to how puppies should ideally be reared, achieving the desired growth rate.

Raising an Irish Wolfhound puppy is an art form, with the science being what you feed, how much and when. Giant breed puppies can be very fragile, and perfecting the careful balance of nutrition and exercise to protect them from injuring themselves can be tricky. By following some simple steps, calamities will be at a minimum!

The other hardest part of raising an Irish Wolfhound is keeping them safe from their exuberance. They grow like weeds, and their bones and joints are just as fragile. Some joint problems can be hereditary, but by the same token, they can also be induced by trauma, poor rearing and overfeeding. It seems a particularly hard message to convey to new puppy owners exactly how important it is to be vigilant in the first year during the growing process.

I take my role as a breeder very seriously; you now have the task of continuing with the correct diet, which is one of the most important factors, the right exercise and keeping your puppy injury free.

TO SUMMARISE THE THREE FACTORS WHICH PLAY AN IMPORTANT PART IN THE REARING AND THE HEALTH OF YOUR PUPPY ARE:

GENETICS, NUTRITION, AND TRAUMA.

Breeding with Love, for Health & Fitness

The Beginning

Looking after puppy's health begins with the nutrition and wellbeing of both parents.

Mum's health, fitness and emotional well being throughout her life are of the utmost importance; the girls have to be fit and healthy to have puppies.

The same ethos also applies to the sire. A sire can produce far more puppies in his lifetime than a bitch. Therefore care must be taken and wise choices made when considering a match.

Once we recognise mum is having puppies we add special food and supplements into her diet, which provides “extra” nutritional support during this physically demanding period.

Mum then stays on this nutritional programme, supporting the high-energy needs of a nursing mother. Besides, this feeding schedule helps the transition from mother's milk to solid food for her puppies.

Once puppies are ready for weaning, or mixed feeding, they continue on the same ingredients mum has been on. It ensures a very simple transition, supporting digestion and supplying their nutritional needs.

Time, care and patience are required to ensure pups are ready for their new homes; it is not a process to be rushed and not all the pups develop at the same rate. Amongst other things they need to be independently feeding, and Mum needs to be independent of them too. The puppies need to have a healthy appetite, growing well and have a good digestion. They also need to be active, well balanced and contented.

At some point during this transitional process of independence, we start feeding puppies on Bonaforte's Complete. They need to be sated, and we need to be satisfied that they are eating and growing well.

Once mum has decided she no longer wishes to feed her pups, we respect her decision. She will always be near them; she may want to check up on them, sniff, clean and maybe teach them a thing or too, but eventually she won't let them feed off her, and we need to have the pups prepared for this time. Mum will continue on her nutritional support even though she is not feeding her pups until she is back to full health and fitness. This process can take up to a year and sometimes longer, and also why mum may or may not have another litter. I hope this explains to you why we are so keen on discussing dietary requirements.

THE CORRECT NUTRITION IS VITAL FOR YOUR HOUND'S BALANCED GROWTH AND WELL-BEING.

Nurture

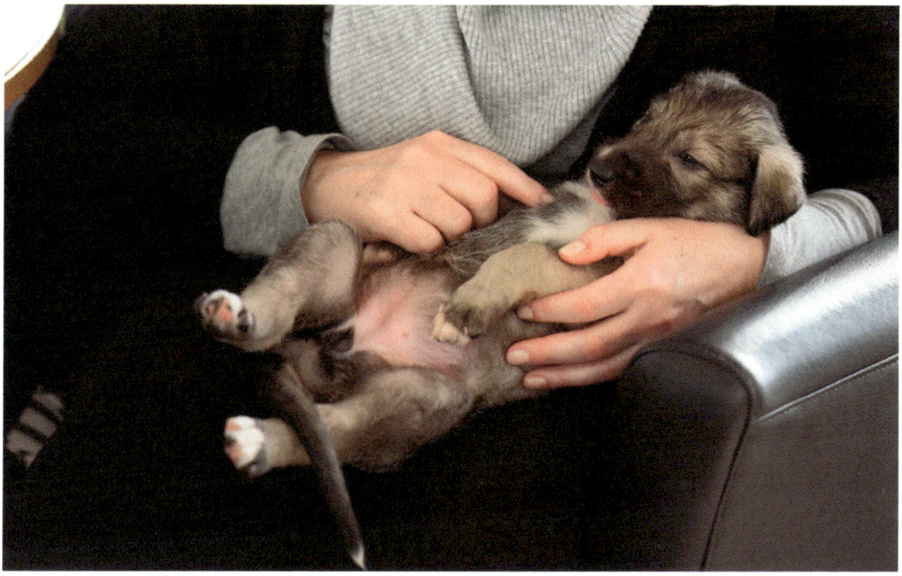

Caring, feeding and protecting puppies is a huge part of raising our litters. The puppies and mum take priority. We constantly sit with mum from before she has her pups until the pups are weaning and she is ready to leave them for a few hours. This care is very intensive, during which we ensure that every need is fulfilled.

Socialisation and handling play a vital role in our rearing techniques, giving our puppies the best possible foundation. They benefit from the complete home experience while growing up. Also, we feel is it paramount that puppies regularly go outside not only to play and exercise but also to help with house training.

Our puppies are used to the vacuum cleaner, washing machine, dishwasher, TV and radio, the general clatter and commotion of the home. We expose them to as many different sounds and new experiences as possible and are keen to introduce them to as many floor surfaces as possible too.

We start with tactile stimulation as soon as they open their eyes, this helps puppy improve its willingness to submit, achieving feelings of affection, comfort, and safety and become more relaxed when touched and held. Our aim is to ensure tasks like grooming, nail clipping, giving medication, examining feet, tail, ears, teeth, etc. are less stressful for the puppy and owner.

AS AN OWNER YOU NEED TO CONTINUE WITH A SOCIALISATION PLAN

CHAPTER 2

Feeding Guide

FEEDING YOUR GROWING IRISH WOLFHOUND FROM PUPPY INTO ADULTHOOD.

Looking after your Irish Wolfhound's diet is one of the most important things you can do, and what you feed and rear on will have an effect on your hound's health and their behaviour for their entire life.

Your hound was built to be an athlete, agile, fit and capable of catching a rabbit; it is your responsibility to ensure you create a balance in your Irish Wolfhound's diet to ensure your hound is fit for purpose.

Keeping the diet simple, fresh, and as natural as possible, is the foundation to a healthy Irish Wolfhound.

Rearing Wolfhound puppies can be tough, and it is a common misconception that a big puppy is a healthy puppy. A slow growing puppy will not affect how large your puppy is in adulthood either. Puppy will still become a giant Wolfhound very quickly. In fact over feeding a puppy during the active, rapid growth period can lead to skeletal problems.

A slow growth diet is prescribed for your puppy to avoid unnecessary orthopaedic problems. Over feeding will encourage limbs to grow too fast, feet to turn out, knuckles to become too large, developing cartilage that can't keep up with the rapid bone growth with too much stress and weight on elbows, and other joints causing damage. If you overfeed this will happen, and it will need correcting before it is too late and the damage caused.

An overweight, chubby hound typically becomes this way by using their soulful eyes to convince you they need your toast in the morning, especially a well-buttered slice, because yes, you end up making them a slice of toast as well! Once you are under their spell, they will continue to convince you that human food is their desire. Be strong!

By the same token don't underfeed them either; bones are constantly remodelling and underfeeding can be more detrimental for future bone strength. Correct nutrition is imperative, to maintain a perfect balance between weight and exercise, protecting their all-important rapid growth of bones and joints.

Here are some guidelines on how to rear your puppy and hopefully to avoid some dietary and health issues:

Steer clear of any complete foods containing Soya, as this blocks absorption in the gut of valuable minerals and is hard to digest if your Irish Wolfhound is sensitive.

Choose a diet as chemically additive free as you can. Yeasts can also cause allergic reactions, so avoid these too along with sugars.

Similarly, try and avoid using all pulses, as they are not only difficult for some to digest, they are often the ingredients which can cause allergic reactions.

A kibble high in grain is very hard to digest and does eventually weaken the digestive system. A high grain based diet is also considered by some to be a cause of bloat. However, rice can also cause issues.

Any change of food, can irritate and cause inflammation in the gut, so please take care when feeding anything other than dog food.

Avoid feeding meat and fruit together as they digest at different rates in the gut. Fruit can also ferment in the gut, so leave a few hours between feeding protein and fruit.

You need to choose the right proteins and do not just rear on milk and Weetabix. Pick a decent hypoallergenic brand such as Bonaforte's Complete and one that isn't full of packers and fillers, or high in minerals.

Some Wolfhounds can be very sensitive, so please give yours the best chance with a good start and sensible diet.

IT IS FORTUNATE THAT YOUR HOUND'S DIET IS SOMETHING WHICH YOU AS AN OWNER HAVE CONTROL OVER. THEIR WELL-BEING IS IN YOUR HANDS.

What to Feed, Why & When

I feed my hounds on Bonaforte's Complete, and I recommend all owners to continue using this brand. It is the control kibble for the entire kennel, and we see some excellent results, regarding heart health, fitness and the correct bone growth. I am always a little concerned when owners change the diet, as I have found it to be tried and tested, benefiting to my hound's all round good health.

The brand has been chosen, as the salmon content is a natural source of the Omega 3 oils, good for heart health, joints and digestion. It is also an excellent source of vitamins, proteins, and essential minerals:

iron, calcium, selenium, phosphorus and vitamins A, B and D.

Potato has many good properties too, containing predominantly carbohydrates, which are easy to digest, contain vitamin-C, potassium and vitamin-B6, amongst others, they help relieve inflammation of intestines and the digestive system.

Apart from the correct amount of vitamins, minerals, and roughage, potatoes also contain certain substances called Carotenoids (lutein, zeaxanthin, etc.) which are beneficial for heart and other internal organs.

Add to this a diet a combination of raw meaty bones, raw chicken wings, raw eggs with shells, fresh carrots (they love to crunch them) and 20 to 30 ml of Olive Oil per day over their food, and this appears to be keeping the kennel healthy and fit.

Please do not feed your puppy any additional supplements, especially calcium, or a diet rich in minerals as this too can lead to problems, especially with bone growth.

I would suggest that you keep your puppy on the diet that they have been used to, allowing a period to settle into their new environment with you. If you wish to change the diet, then do it gradually. Personally, as stated above, I avoid feeding soya, sugar and any legumes, as these can be hard to digest for some and can create wind. Always check your dog's poo, as much as you can, as this is a good indication of their digestive system.

Puppy will need at least three meals per day, possibly four until a little older. We have given the first feed around 07.30hrs, the second feed around Midday, the third around 16.00hrs and the last feed between 19.30hrs to 20.00hrs. You, of course, can alter these times to suit your routines.

We place an amount of the kibble, mixed with a little Grain Free in the bowl and if this is eaten up, then we put another handful until the puppy is sated. Don't forget to top with a little Olive Oil.

Regarding the amount to feed a puppy, it's hard to be very prescriptive as each puppy is an individual and will require a different level of food to meet its energy needs and its size and gender. Typically the boys will eat more than their female siblings as they will always be bigger than their female counterparts, but some puppies are lazy with their food whereas others can be very greedy. As a general guideline, your puppy for the first few weeks should not be eating more than around 400g of Complete per day, and the only way to be accurate about this is to weigh the food using kitchen scales – never trust your eye as a guide to food quantities!

AN AVERAGE PUPPY FEEDING REGIME FOR THE 8 TO 14 WEEKS STAGE SHOULD LOOK SOMETHING LIKE THIS:

07:30hrs 100g Bonaforte's Complete

12:00hrs 100g Bonaforte's Complete

16:00hrs 100g Bonaforte's Complete

20:00hrs 100g Bonaforte's Complete

When your puppy starts leaving food uneaten then it is the right time to reduce from 4 meals per day to 3 meals per day, and typically the lunchtime feed is the one that is stopped, so a puppy on 3 meals per day would have a feeding regime something like this:

07:30hrs 150g Bonaforte's Complete

15:00hrs 150g Bonaforte's Complete

21:00hrs 100g Bonaforte's Complete

At all times monitor poo, you are looking for nicely formed ones! If your puppy/youngster scours, (diarrhoea) due to an imbalance in the diet, just go back to feeding the Complete. If the scouring is for other reasons, seek veterinary advice.

OVERFEEDING A PUPPY DURING THE ACTIVE, RAPID GROWTH PERIOD LEADS TO SKELETAL PROBLEMS.

OVERFEEDING AN ADULT DOG WILL LEAD TO OBESITY AND SERIOUS HEALTH CONDITIONS SUCH AS DIABETES AND HEART DISEASE.

Drinks.

Irish Wolfhounds love to not only drink loads of cool fresh water and wipe their wet, cold beard on you afterwards, but they also love to splash around in their water bowls and send the contents flying.

You will need to become creative and find ways of securing their water source. We recommend that you have a bucket or large water receptacle outside and ensure this is kept full. However just be aware that outside buckets and troughs need to be kept clean and free from slugs (they carry lung worm) and worms etc.. Top tip; add a good splash of cider vinegar to maintain the water algae and bug-free. Apple Cider Vinegar is also purportedly good for all kinds of conditions.

YOUR HOUND MUST ALWAYS HAVE ACCESS TO LOTS OF CLEAN FRESH WATER

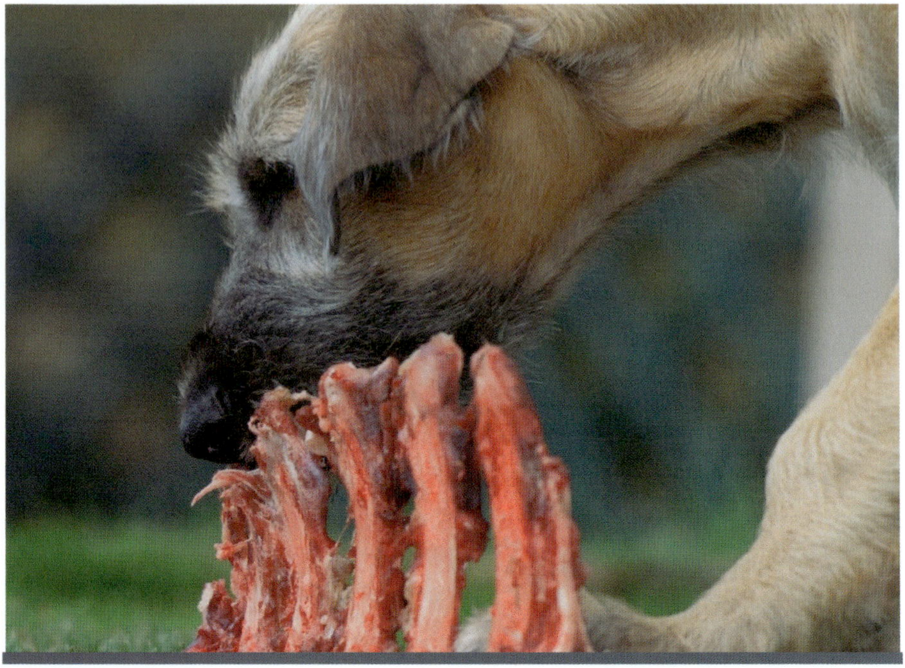

CHAPTER 3

Feeding at Home

Puppy may or may not eat at first after their journey home, but they will not starve. Puppies leave us content with their food, however once at home with you, you may experience a mini hunger strike. Puppy is emotionally adjusting to their new surrounds. Persevere with love and hugs: They have just left their brothers and sisters along with the routines and smells they have known since birth. Give them a day or two to settle in, and by mixing a little taste of tinned fish, it can help them regain an appetite.

Your puppy will grow very quickly so always feed Bonaforte's Complete to appetite, ensuring there is always a little something left in the bowl. If the puppy has loose stools from a change of diet, or over eating, just revert to feeding Bonaforte's Complete until they firm up.

There is no need to modify the diet; this food takes them all the way into adulthood and their senior years. If you do decide to change the feeding plan, please don't try to modify the diet all in one go! Doing so can invoke all kinds of unpleasant digestive issues!

A SLOW GROWTH FOOD IS OF VITAL IMPORTANCE FOR YOUR PUPPY TO AVOID ORTHOPAEDIC PROBLEMS.

Puppy Menu

BONAFORTE'S COMPLETE

BONAFORTE'S GRAIN FREE

Salmon, Trout, Sweet Potato, & Asparagus

As puppy matures, you can add in the other Grain Free options.

HELPS ACTIVE PUPS KEEP CONDITION BUT WITHOUT RAPID GROWTH

Extras

THESE INGREDIENTS ARE NEW TO PUPPY BUT CAN BE ADDED TO THEIR DIET IF YOU WISH

LIVE YOGHURT With Honey
GOATS MILK: is especially useful if the weather has been hot and they don't feel like eating - it has a high calorific content though, but low-fat options are available. Don't grow puppy on this; it is the wrong kind of protein.

SARDINES/PILCHARDS / SALMON / IN OIL/BRINE
FRESH FRUIT AS A TREAT - APPLES, BANANAS
FRESH VEGETABLES - Especially Carrots

RAW EGGS IN SHELLS
SCRAMBLED EGGS IN COCONUT OIL
RAW MEATY BONES, - ones, which don't splinter and do not feed pork bones.

NEVER EXERCISE YOUR WOLFHOUND ONE HOUR BEFORE OR 2 HOURS AFTER FEEDING OR IF YOU ARE CHANGING YOUR KIBBLE, ALWAYS CHANGE SLOWLY FOR FEAR OF BLOATING

Size Check

Many owners contact us in the first few weeks concerned that they may be overfeeding or underfeeding their puppy and usually their first reaction is to quote the puppy's body weight. While body weight is a good indication of whether the puppy (or indeed an adult dog) is healthy, differences in height, gender, bone mass, growth stages and even bloodlines will render such measurements to being less indicative.

Standing over the top of your puppy and looking down at their back, you should be able to see the puppy's shoulders, then a slight tuck in before the tummy and following the line of the puppy back towards the tail there should be a waist visible. The body should then tuck in again after the end of the ribcage and flare out slightly where the hips emerge – see pictures 2 and 3 for details. Also, by running your hand along the side of your puppy's body, the ribs should be easily felt without having to 'dig' around for them. While image 3 is classed as 'ideal' body condition, it is also perfectly acceptable for a giant breed puppy to be slightly underweight, as in picture 2 above. Just like humans, dog too can suffer from being too fat or even obese, and for a giant breed puppy such as a Wolfhound, the effects of being overweight can be disastrous! If your puppy appears overweight, you must take steps to rectify the situation and start by cutting out all dietary extras and go back to the Bonaforte's Complete and reduce the quantity of kibble fed.

The Pet Food Manufacturer's Association has produced a useful visual guide to evaluating your puppy or adult dog's general body condition.

Dog Size-O-Meter

Size-O-Meter Score:		Characteristics:
1	**Very Thin** More than 20% below ideal body weight	• Ribs, spine and hip bones are very easily seen (in short haired pets) • Obvious loss of muscle bulk • No fat can be felt under the skin
2	**Thin** Between 10-20% below ideal body weight	• Ribs, spine and hip bones easily seen • Obvious waist and abdominal tuck • Very little fat can be felt under the skin
3	**Ideal**	• Ribs, spine and hip bones easily felt • Visible waist with an abdominal tuck • A small amount of fat can be felt
4	**Overweight** 10-15% above ideal body weight	• Ribs, spine and hip bones are hard to feel • Waist bearly visible with a broad back • Layer of fat on belly and at base of tail
5	**Obese** More than 15% above ideal body weight	• Ribs, spine and hip bones extremely difficult to feel under a thick layer of fat • No waist can be seen and belly may droop significantly • Heavy fat pads on lower back and at the base of the tail

Derived from BCSC validated by: Keely, et al. Effects of diet restriction on life span and age related changes in dogs. JAVMA 2002.
Laflamme DP. Development and validation of a body condition score system for dogs. Canine Practice. July/August 1997, 22:10-15
Mawby D. Bartges JW, Moyers, T et al. Comparison of body fat estimates by dual-energy x-ray absorptiometry and deuterium oxide dilution in client owned dogs.

- Your pet is a healthy weight
- Seek advice about your pet's weight
- Seek advice as your pet could be at risk

Please note
There are some cases where the natural shape of a dog may mean this simple system doesn't translate as easily. For example, Whippets and Greyhounds tend to have lean physiques while a Staffie will have a broader shape. A Bichon Frisé will have a nice fluffy coat for you to contend with. If you need help using the tool, download a hard copy version and take it to your local vet or pet care professional for advice.

pfma
pet food manufacturers' association
www.pfma.org.uk

Check out our top 5 tips for feeding your dog.

1. Clean, fresh water should always be available
2. Read the feeding guidelines on the pet food packet. Use these as a starting point but you may need to adapt the amount fed depending on your dog's age and how active he/she is.
3. Monitor your dog's weight and body condition regularly - use our Dog Size-O-Meter to check your pet's size and shape. When you are happy with their body condition, then note their weight.
4. Be careful when feeding treats; these are extra calories that need to be taken into consideration at mealtimes.
5. Treating with human foods should be avoided – they are often too high in calories for pets. Did you know that 1 cookie for a medium sized breed of dog provides a similar calorie level as 2 cookies for a person?

Remember to make the most of advice on weight management offered by many vet practices and pet care professionals.

pfma
pet food manufacturers' association
www.pfma.org.uk

Dog Size-O-Meter

Results:		
Your Dog is score **Very Thin**	1	Your pet is very likely to be underweight. Your pet may have a naturally lean physique but we recommend you speak to your local vet to rule out any underlying medical reasons such as an overactive thyroid gland. If your pet is healthy but otherwise underweight, your vet is likely to advise some dietary and lifestyle changes.
Your Dog is score **Thin**	2	Your pet is thin and potentially underweight. Your pet may have a naturally lean physique but we recommend you speak to your local vet for a health check up. If your pet is healthy but otherwise underweight, your vet may advise some dietary and lifestyle changes.
Your Dog is score **Ideal**	3	Congratulations your pet is in ideal body condition! This is great news, as research has shown that pets at their ideal body condition can live up to two years longer. To keep your dog in perfect shape, monitor its weight and body condition on a regular basis (eg. reduced exercise, recent surgery, extra treats, or even factors such as stress) can result in weight change.
Your Dog is score **Overweight**	4	Your pet is potentially overweight. Being overweight is unhealthy for pets as it can lead to a shortened life-span, heart disease, arthritis and diabetes. Speak to your local vet for advice and a thorough health check-up. The vet will look for any underlying health issues, a change of diet and lifestyle is likely to be suggested. Many vet practices run free weight management consultations, ask about these services when you ring to book an appointment.
Your Dog is score **Obese**	5	Your pet is likely to be obese and this can have serious medical implications. Being overweight is unhealthy for pets as it can lead to a shortened life-span, heart disease, arthritis and diabetes. Speak to your local vet for advice and a thorough health check-up. The vet will look for any underlying medical reasons as to why your pet may be too heavy. If there are no underlying health issues, a weight loss programme will probably be individually developed for your pet and should include diet and lifestyle changes.

For more information on the Dog Size-O-Meter and tips on how to prevent weight gain visit **www.pfma.org.uk**. In addition to providing useful tips on how to keep your pet healthy and happy, a team of veterinary nutrition experts are on hand to answer your pet nutrition questions in the 'Ask the Expert' section.

Possessive of Food

When dogs live as a pack, they have a pecking order and your puppy, for the first weeks of its life, will have had the protection of its mother and her ranking.

When puppy enters your pack, i.e. your family, you must ensure that puppy knows his place in the pack's (family's) ranking order. Puppy must, therefore, learn that all humans have a higher ranking than it has.

The last thing you want is for your dog to start playing boss, starting to protect what it considers to belong to him, i.e. "its" food, "its" toy or "its" bed. The last thing you want is to be bossed around by a dog who thinks he is in charge. What steps can you take to prevent this from happening?

- You eat first - this is what occurs in a pack, the alpha dog always eats first.

- Feed your dog at a set time each day - preferably a quiet time.
- Make your dog wait quietly for their food.
- Ensuring they go into the sit position.
- Place food in the bowl.
- Hold the bowl in front of the dog, but you pretend to eat.
- To ensure also that the dog recognises you as the pack leader has eaten, lightly spit in the bowl on the food, thus leaving your scent on the food.
- Providing your dog is sitting and calm, place the food down on the floor - holding on to the bowl. Do not allow him to eat until you say so.
- Remove the food bowl once he has finished and walked away.
- Don't feed at the food table as this breaks the pack code.

Repeat this until you feel confident that your dog knows that you are in charge.

I hope this helps you understand how your dog thinks, and by understanding, you can help him. He is just acting out his natural instincts, and his mum would not let him get away with such an attitude and neither should you.

HELP PUPPY RE-FOCUS AND ESTABLISH HIS TRUE ORDER IN THE FAMILY. THE FAMILY PET.

CHAPTER 4

RUPERT - HIS FIRST FEW MONTHS

01/01/2017 - Rupert weighed 14.5kg, and we fed him on:

200g of Bonaforte's Complete 3x daily plus 100g at suppertime.

Feed times were roughly-7am, 12 noon, 5 pm and supper at 8 pm.

Plain live yoghurt with honey once a day and an apple.

Also, a marrowbone twice a day to chew. It is proven that eating a bone releases endorphins for dogs and it is good for a puppy to have something to do. It also means you can start training the puppy to give it back and not be possessive over food. With Rupert, we did this by offering a high-value treat (a bit of sausage) after 15mins of chewing the bone. He naturally looked up when approached and was offered the treat, as he took it we picked the bone up. In his mind, it created a positive experience, and we have had no food issues and can take anything off him at meal times. We also stood next to puppy while eating and dropped some biscuits into the bowl and stroke them, they get used to you being present and no threat to taking the food away. You eliminate the need for them to "guard" their food.

House training - You have to be with them watching and make sure that they toilet outside and give them lots of praise if they do. When they have an accident, just clean it up without reacting and go outside with them every time to toilet.

Bedtime-establish a bedtime routine straight away. Rupert had an enormous crate-bedding inside but also a huge teddy and a hot water bottle wrapped in a towel. Creating warmth as the puppy is used to sleeping with siblings. The last toilet at 11 pm and up at 6 am to start the day.

12/02/2017 - Rupert weighed 19.6kg

At this stage the owner adds in tripe, to Rupert's diet, she knows my personal feelings on this! You can instead increase the Bonaforte's Complete by 50 to 100g. Adding in the oily fish, or raw chicken wings if you wish and olive oil, or just feed the Complete as we do in the Kennel.

Rupert still has 200g Bonaforte's Complete 3x times a day but added 100g green tripe to every meal.

Yoghurt and honey once a day and an apple.

Rupert is very clean and has not had any toilet accidents, and this is due to my being at home and watching all the signs he makes he will now also at times walk to the door and ask to go out.

He enjoys a chew on a marrow bone still twice a day and happily gives it up when he has finished. I still drop biscuits into his bowl when he is eating we also have taught him to sit using treats, and he will sit when it's time for his meals.

Play time is kept to the garden, and his interaction with the adults is limited and supervised. Another Wolfhound treading on a puppy can cause tremendous damage so always err on the side of caution.

Introducing the collar - I followed the advice given in Gwen Bailey's puppy book and Rupert accepted his collar with no trauma. It may distress some, so take your time with this process.

Rupert does not have water in the crate at night and he is totally clean.

26/01/2017 - Rupert weighed 23.7kg.

Rupert still on 200g Complete and 150g of tripe per meal plus yoghurt apple.

Training treats are tiny bits of sausage or chicken. We now use a lead and take him in the garden to get him used to walk on the lead he is very playful and can do sit-down-and off. He is clean in the house.

We encourage visitors to get him used to people, and he is confident and happy to meet people. He has also had his full vaccinations so can now go out. However, I choose to take this slowly.

07/02/2017 - Rupert weighed 25kg

Rupert is now a big puppy, and extra care is taken with exercise. He is still just playing in the garden and supervised interaction with the adults as he wants to play and is quite rough, so stepping in and making sure he knows what is and isn't acceptable

Car-time: to get him out in the car I put his big teddy in the car for comfort and took him to the vets, no fuss made, just put him in and off he travelled well and settled. By keeping everything calm, he accepts things easily. I have discussed with the vet that I will take him every week/fortnight to be weighed so he is happy to go to vets and not be frightened. He is very pleased to meet people.

16/02/2017 - Rupert weighed 29.8kg

250g Complete plus 150g tripe 3 x times a day. Yoghurt and honey and apple. Marrow bone to chew on.

Rupert has started puppy classes. It is vital to socialise your puppy they are going to be huge dogs and need to be friendly and happy to meet all sorts of people/dogs.

Rupert is put into his crate twice a day to rest in the morning for at least 2hrs and in the afternoon for another 2hrs. He tends to sleep, but it is vital to rest your puppy. The growth rate puts a tremendous strain on the puppy's skeleton, and rest is a massive part of rearing. The play is kept to the garden. Rupert is now ripping all of his toys to bits. The hunt is on for toys that can withstand him, as yet nothing has. Be aware of teething he gets hot ears, and his feet have gone flat, some days he has quiet days and sleeps a lot more all normal. I take Rupert out on the lead for a short walk to the top of the road to watch traffic go by-to get him used to noise and traffic.

01/03/2017 - Rupert weighed 34.5kg

250g Complete 200g, tripe, yoghurt and honey apple/carrot lamb bone. I have started Rupert on a lamb rib carcass. I supervise, but he is doing very well with it. I take it off him when it gets quite small. He is happy to give up bones/toys etc

Rupert continues to do well, very pleased as he is a confident puppy, he is excellent at puppy training, though apparently bored, it means he is around other dogs, in particular, small yappy dogs, and he is nonreactive. He is still teething, and being a little destructive around the house. We are still keeping any exercise to a controlled minimum, and he still is crate rested twice a day.

05/05/2017 - Rupert weighed 49.5kg

Rupert is now 6.5months old. He is now on 350g Complete and 250g of tripe per meal 3x times daily.

He has a lot more interaction with the adults and has formed close bonds with them. He goes out for an on the lead walk daily and has some playtime in the garden. He still goes to training, but it is for socialisation. He understands basic commands-sit-down-stay-heel and is a very happy friendly puppy.

Raising a Wolfhound puppy is like having porcelain in a furry coat.

Amanda likes feeding tripe, you can if you wish, but it obviously has no nutritional value, unless green and straight from the abattoir. It does, however, help make the food smell, and their beard, and maybe they love the taste of it. I would suggest you increase the Bonaforte's Complete and omit the tripe, tasting the kibble with tinned oily fish if you wish. - Carla

CHAPTER 5

Exercise - Less is More

With a new puppy, too much exercise and the incorrect exercise can inadvertently cause more harm than good. Over walking and over exercising your puppy in the first year can cause life long injuries.

Care must be taken during the first 12 months at least before you can take these long walks together.

Firstly you must look at your hound puppy and realise that to become a giant; there is a lot of growing to be accomplished. However the problem is while they are growing and becoming giants they are still puppies, enormous puppies, and far from being mature enough to avoid simple injuries.

WHAT KIND OF EXERCISE IS BEST?

Free play is the best play for your puppy. Exploring the garden, and pottering around, until tired and flops down. Listen to pup at this point, they will tell you when they are tired, and always be there to supervise; they can't just race around all day. Puppies need plenty of rest.

WHAT KIND OF EXERCISE IS NOT GOOD?

Repetitive exercise is bad! So no long walks, just lots of free play. Take the opportunity and incorporate some training and keep puppy busy, both in mind and body. Short bursts of positive training with rewards can quickly tire your puppy out.

WHAT ABOUT A PLAY-MATE?

A well-matched companion is always good, but choose wisely, not one who gives puppy huge paw whacks and not one who likes to body swipe or one who encourages the puppy to twist and turn, or slip and slide, as these can cause injuries. Smaller playmates can be far too agile to be permitted to play with young puppies. Don't let your puppy play with other dogs unsupervised, even if they are your dogs and are playing at home. A Wolfhound puppy does not need to play with older or larger dogs until it is at least a year old. A breeder would never allow this. We always keep the youngsters separate from the older hounds.

WHAT ABOUT GETTING OUT OF THE CAR, OFF THE SOFA OR OFF THE BED?

Basically, care should be taken with any activity, which in effect puts pressure on legs and joints.

High impact activities such as jumping off anything, including the sofa, the bed, or any piece of furniture, jumping out of the car, along with bounding up and down steps and stairs, and walking for too long, are not good.

HIGH IMPACT ACTIVITIES ARE ONE OF THE MAJOR CAUSES OF

STRESS FRACTURES, SPIRAL FRACTURES AND DAMAGE TO GROWTH PLATES-

With any activity, which in effect puts pressure on legs and joints, you need to be vigilant.

High impact activities such as jumping off anything, including the sofa, the bed, or any piece of furniture, jumping out of the car, along with bounding up and down steps and stairs, and walking for too long, are not safe.

High impact activities are one of the principal causes of stress fractures, spiral fractures and damage to growth plates and joints.

Avoid movement, which creates an impact on the growth plates or joints, especially elbows or a twist of a joint at all costs. Your growing puppy needs a soft cushioned and aided landing when getting off the sofa or bed! Or better still provide a flat soft, comfy dog bed for them to enjoy.

When rearing a giant breed, there is the potential for a lot of problems, which can make the first year very time-consuming. Their long legs are prone to injury, during their rapid and prolonged growth phase. Many of the issues associated with lameness and joints are due to the actual way the legs are constructed. There are soft areas of cartilage at the end of their long bones (Growth Plates), which are weak, vulnerable areas.

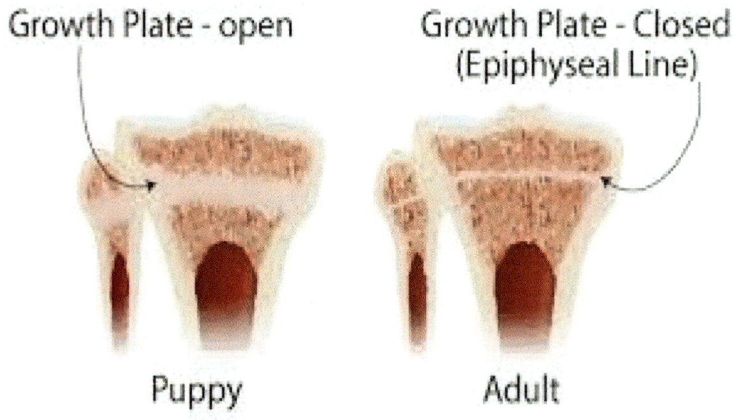

The growth plates are soft because they allow for the bones to grow longer and gradually these growth plates, thin and harden. However, the problem is, they don't harden until puberty has finished (probably due to the hormone changes), and puberty can be a long time coming in a giant breed. Puppies' muscles, ligaments, and tendons are far stronger than the soft growth plates and therefore will not take the impact of any injury.

In addition to soft growth plates, puppy also has fragile bones, and this leads to all kinds of injuries when growing. Twists and turns, and jumping out of the car or off furniture can put undue pressure on the lower leg bone (tibia) and lead to fractures, especially spiral fractures which are quite common in puppies.

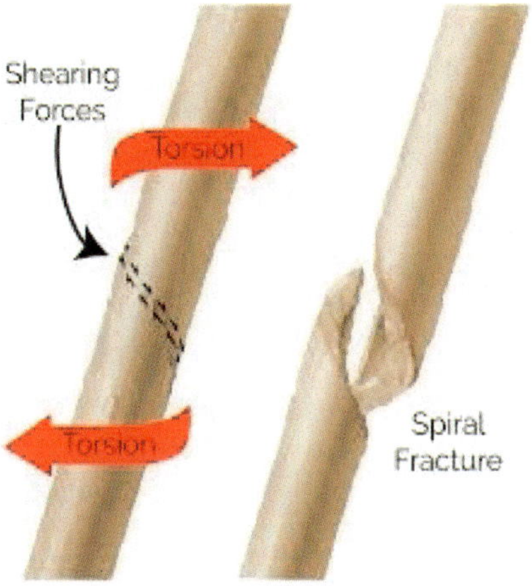

Therefore your puppy can seriously be harmed by twisting, turning and jumping. If the growth plate is damaged, it may not be possible for it to heal in time for puppy's legs to grow correctly. Such an injury can result in a shortened limb or a wrong angle to a joint. If this kind of injury happens to a large hound, it can have a detrimental effect on the way they continue to grow and cause untold suffering, pain, deformities and long-term problems.

During these formative months, the growth plates and soft bones are vulnerable to injury, and this is why it is your responsibility to restrict and supervise exercise as required, and why we keep repeating ourselves to new owners.

THINK WITH CARE AND BEFORE YOU EXERCISE YOUR PUPPY

Which Exercise is Best ?

Free play is the best play for your puppy. Exploring the garden, and pottering around, until tired and flops down. Listen at this point; puppy will tell you when tired and always be there to supervise play.

- Do allow your puppy free exercise in a secure area preferably on grass every day. Although giant breed puppies have fragile bones and joints, they do require some exercise to build up muscle tone and stamina. A supervised run around on a dry lawn, (not wet slippery grass), with you keeping an eye on them is imperative.

- Do take your puppy out to meet people and other dogs once fully vaccinated. Socialising your puppy is paramount, and any dog needs to get used to new places and experiences such as going in the car to visit friends and family or going to the park to meet other dogs and puppy class.

SUPERVISED FREE PLAY IS BEST

The Big DO's and DON'Ts

The most difficult thing about raising an Irish Wolfhound is keeping them safe from their exuberance. New owners find it difficult to understand that the right care is vital for the first year during the growing process. As a breeder, it one of the most sensitive messages to convey; I also find it heartbreaking when I hear of accidents which could have been avoided. You need to perfect the careful balance of nutrition and exercise to protect them.

Follow these simple steps to avoid disasters, or at least try and keep them to a minimum!

DO:

- Do feed your puppy on a healthy balanced diet. We advise you feed Bonaforte's Complete. Poor nutrition or over feeding can lead to problems.
- Do allow your puppy free exercise in a secure area preferably on grass (which isn't wet and slippery) every day. Although giant breed puppies have fragile bones and joints, they do require some exercise to build up muscle tone and stamina and so a run around on a dry lawn with their owner keeping an eye on them is important.
- Do provide a safe and secure place for the puppy to rest, away from other dogs or children.
- Do take your puppy out to meet people and other dogs once fully vaccinated. Socialising your puppy is paramount, and any dog needs to get used to new places and experiences such as going in the car to visits friends and family or going to the park to meet other dogs

DON'T:

- Don't over exercise your puppy under any circumstances. Do not walk your Wolfhound puppy until six months old and then build up the walk gradually, initially only walking for 5 to 10 minutes. Despite their size, Wolfhound puppies are very delicate so treat their growing bones and joints with great care. Any mistakes in exercise and over exuberance under a year old can affect the puppy for the rest of its life.

- Don't let your puppy walk on slippery surfaces such as tiles, laminate flooring, wood flooring or cushion flooring/ lino. Slippery floors are responsible for an enormous amount of injuries in both puppies and older dogs of all breeds, but giant breed puppies are particularly susceptible to mishaps. They will slide on these slippery surfaces and hurt their legs and other parts of their body. Some of these injuries can have disastrous consequences.

- Don’t let your puppy play with other dogs (or children) unsupervised, even if they are your dogs and playing at home. Do not let a Wolfhound puppy play with older/larger dogs until it is at least a year old. Or even a smaller active breed, which twists and turns in the chase. Again, letting your puppy run riot with other dogs is likely to end up with the puppy being hurt or injured.
- Don’t let your puppy walk up and down stairs, and prevent them from jumping out of cars. Keep impact on all joints to a minimum, even getting on and off sofas in an exuberant manner may harm.
- Don't let puppy run over rough ground and fields. These areas can be fraught with potholes and hidden obstacles, which may cause the puppy to stumble and tumble and hurt those long fragile limbs.

CHAPTER 6

Training

A frequently asked question is "are Irish Wolfhounds easy to train?" My first answer is well "yes" and "no" to which I immediately add “your dog is only as good as the person on the other end of the lead.”

The Irish Wolfhound is, as you know, a large, strong, and determined dog and if he wants to get on the sofa and stay there and unlike a small pooch, you will find it a struggle to heft him off. He is also a sighthound, and if he is chasing his quarry, it is more than likely he will not hear his recall. It is you who shoulders the responsibility of this; he is just following his instincts. So it is paramount to start with some very basic training of your Irish Wolfhound puppy, it will make life easier for you both.

It is not difficult to train your Irish Wolfhound puppy/dog, however, whichever method you choose, what is required is persistence, patience and repeated practice. Apply to the pair of you, and your dog will unconditionally reflect your ability.

Firstly you need to decide who in the family is responsible for the dog training.

Dogs are notoriously quick at picking up on family power struggles and will exploit these to their own end. All non-executive family trainers should be just that and wait for you to issue your training manual! Secondly, decide as the instructor, and in discussion with other family members, what the boundaries are, what you want and expect from your hound, how much time you want to give to training and the level of response required in return.

I have developed my commands and techniques over the years. I try to keep things simple and train what is necessary to make all our lives easy. I use simple commands and signs which not only can I communicate to the dog, but also to other family members. Too many trainers will confuse a dog as they start receiving conflicting commands. I also realised that shouting, yelling and repeatedly giving my dog a command and not obtaining a response, was a sign of my failure. My dogs have perfect sight, more than perfect hearing and hardly ever miss a movement.

Selective deafness is a sign of pushing my boundaries. I had a dog who wherever he was, he could hear the refrigerator door open and would appear. However, you could call him until you were blue in the face and he wouldn't come. We eventually worked this out, and the door was used to our advantage.

Start by thinking and choosing your simple signs and signals for each command and for each task you wish your Wolfhound puppy to do. Once you have decided, stay with them. There are standards signs and commands you can find in most dog training books or like me use a mish mash of what suits.

Come/five blasts on a whistle/ hand clapping/finger clicks - are all my recall commands.

Sit/index finger held up/or pressure from hand at the top of the tail/ - are all my sit commands.

Down/click of fingers and point index finger down to the ground - are my down commands.

No/Ah Ah - are my stop leave that alone commands, delivered in a commanding tone.

In/Out- are self-explanatory, and especially useful for getting dogs in and out of cars and through doorways, before and after closing doors.

"Off" is a must with a Wolfie, as in "get off the sofa."

Also, add the dog's name at the beginning or end of these commands, to begin with, this is helpful if more than one dog is involved.

Irish Wolfhound training starts with the bonding on the way home in the car and the minute you get home you need to start training. When holding your puppy keep saying their name. If you get down on your hands and knees, a puppy will always come to you, call their name and say come at the same time. This is a double learning experience.

Sit, is the next easy command to teach. Using mealtime is an excellent opportunity to teach this. Hold the feed bowl up and over your dog's head while saying sit, the dog naturally looks at the bowl, bottom goes down and sits. Keep repeating this ritual every time you feed. Once the puppy is sitting on voice command, you can then eventually use just your index finger as a command to sit. Silent commands and proper responses are very satisfying. As soon as you can, add blowing a whistle, five short blasts when their food is prepared, this is the beginning of my outdoor re-call signal. I have found shouting your dog's name, or come in the field against the wind can be a thankless task sometimes, but five short blasts on a whistle never fail to work. Keep repeating this before feeding and add to outside play times, and use your favourite dog treat as the reward of a positive response.

House training your Irish Wolfhound puppy starts the minute you get home too. If you are struggling and puppy won't house train, this is in fact your fault. Puppies and dogs hate messing their space. You have to be disciplined in your approach to this, having regular meal times and regular going out times after eating, drinking, waking and exercising.

I like to keep the pups in a large pen in the kitchen, as I find this an easier method of toilet training. They are safe; they are not running around all over the house getting excited and messing. The pen soon becomes a relaxing, safe space for you all. A safe place to eat, to drink, to have toys, and to sleep. I let the puppy out of the pen, out we go; he runs around and plays in the kitchen, out we go; he eats and out we go; he drinks and out we go; he wakes up and out we go. He meets new people in the kitchen, and out we go. Noticed the "we" have you? Well, it pays off in the end, and as I have said once before, your dog is only as good as it's trainer. One small tip here, when you take you dog out and while he is mid flow doing his business, just keep repeating, "hurry quickly" or similar words. These commands will pay dividends for the times later on when you are in a hurry to leave the house, cold nights, or before long car journeys, your dog will know what is expected and get a move on doing his business.

If your puppy is chewing everything in sight, this again is your fault, because you are leaving him things out to chew. Scoop everything up you don't want to be chewed and leave your puppy or dog with something made for him to chew i.e. raw meaty bones, deer antler, or other pet chews. Animals naturally teethe and often require gnawing to aid this along and with keeping their teeth clean and gums healthy.

There is a lot of help out there if you wish to further the training. Training your dog can be very rewarding. Some are easier to train, some are a bit slower, and some need

more time to think about a command. They all have varying degrees of intelligence and response - just like us humans! You will need to assess your dog's ability and
work together accordingly.

Your Irish Wolfhound puppy will reflect back at you, so be calm, be focussed, be grounded, be consistent and be kind. Always reward good responses, this will reap you your rewards.

IRISH WOLFHOUNDS ARE SENSITIVE CREATURES AND RESPOND WELL TO LOVE AND KINDNESS.

Amichien Bonding

A NON-INVASIVE, CALMING APPROACH TO REHABILITATING DOGS AND TRAINING OWNERS, AS POPULARISED BY JAN FENNELL - THE DOGLISTENER

Dog training and the different methods popularised over the decades are like many aspects of dog ownership; there are conventional and less traditional methods, all of which have their followers and their dissenters, but it is a case of "one size does not fit all". Numerous dog owners regularly voice their frustration over some aspects of their dogs' behaviour, such as the dog pulling on the lead, not coming back when called, jumping up, being aggressive towards other dogs or becoming anxious when their owner is out of sight or away from home. Wolfhounds are no exceptions to the usual dilemmas of dog ownership, but the issues can be somewhat exaggerated, not only by the sheer size and scale of a Wolfhound but particularly of the Breed's sensitivity to the mood and behaviour of their owners. This heightened sensitivity, when coupled with the natural intelligence of the Breed, can manifest in negative ways that cause friction between dog and owner.

Amichien Bonding is the straightforward and efficient method of communicating with your dog, in a language it instinctively understands, that you are the dependable leader and decision maker of your "pack."

Although Amichien Bonding may have fallen out of favour in recent years, it can still offer help and assistance to trainers, owners and dogs and create a balanced and harmonious household and lifestyle for all concerned. Having spent time with horse whisperer, Monty Roberts, Jan Fennell devised her system of training based on 4 fundamental principles and her studies of wolf packs showed her that often owners unwittingly reinforce the dog as leader of the pack, rather than the humans:

1. Provision of Food - the alpha pair always eats first

2. Leading the Hunt - the alpha pair are always in front when hunting

3. Protecting the Pack - it is the responsibility of the alphas

4. Reuniting after Separation - the alphas are given space and respect

HOW DO THE 4 PRINCIPLES TRANSLATE INTO EVERYDAY LIFE?

Amichien Bonding maintains that the 4 principles of wolf packs above translate into modern-day life in 4 easy ways:

- Owners must always eat first, before the dog.
- Owners go in and out of the door in front of the dog.

- Owners decide/dictate when the dog gets affection/attention and not the dog.

Ignored when reunited with their owners, and the dog is not given any fuss, spoken to or even looked at when owners come back home or come back into contact with the dog.

To put simply, on an average day, when you first get up, and you see your dog again, you ignore them completely - no touch, no talk, no eye contact (to quote dog trainer, Cesar Milan). You carry on about your business until the dog has become calm and has gone to lie down and rest and typically you can hear the dog give a loud 'sigh' which signals acceptance. At this point, you can call the dog to you to give fuss and affection. Already, as an owner, you have already complied with principles 3 and 4 of Amichien Bonding. Once you have eaten your breakfast, you may then feed the dog, thus complying with the first principle. Breakfast over with and you get ready for the day and probably at some point it is time for your dog to be walked and this is another key moment in the day of your dog. You must ensure that the dog is calm and settled before attempting to put a collar and lead on, so if the dog becomes excited, wait calmly, ignoring whatever the dog is doing until such time that the dog becomes calm again and then, and only then, put on the collar and lead. If your dog becomes excited once again because of having a collar and lead on, then wait for them to calm down. If you are struggling with getting your dog to calm down, try ignoring them by averting your eyes from them, folding your arms and turning your body away. Once the dog is calmly waiting with collar and lead on then make them wait while you open the door and do not let them go running out in front of you - instead, you step out of the door ahead of the dog and then invite them to join you.

Starting the walk in this way then dictates the behaviour and tone for the rest of the walk. You will be pleasantly surprised at just how much that positive action has a knock-on effect for dogs that frequently pull on the lead or lunge at distractions when out walking. The dog will be more focused and compliant, but always be vigilant that your dog walks by your side and does not walk slightly in front of you. A minor lead correction should be all that is needed to ensure that the dog is kept in line with you when walking and dogs, like horses, should learn the technique of 'pressure and release' when out on a lead. The technique works, no matter what the type or style of collar. If you prefer to use a bridle/ head collar (such as a Halti or Dogmatic), then it is easier to fit the dog with a neck collar to apply pressure and release and attach the lead to both collars simultaneously.

Almost all problems arise from a misunderstanding. Once we appreciate that the dog is looking for a leader who cares for them, is kind to them and will step up to the role of leader when they experience concern or fear, we can bring magic to this relationship, with the mere adoption of a four-part information system.

The 4 principles are repeated at every opportunity, both at home and when out, and incorporated into the life of a dog at any age and no matter how many dogs are in the household. The technique is more of a way of life than a one-off training method that is taught at training school and practised at home. As Amichien Bonding does not require owners to be particularly assertive, dominant or physically strong, then it can be utilised to great effect by just about anyone and is very attractive to owners who lack the self-confidence to conquer other techniques. It does not require any expensive equipment, it is not any more time-consuming than your typical day would demand, it does not require attendance at a training class or private tuition by a training professional, and yet it is a process that an owner can continually learn from and the results are instant.

Training Treats

The liver cake is a delicious treat and training aid for your Irish Wolfhound. The Happy Hounds here just love it, improving their recall when out in the field - In fact when they smell this they don't venture far.

Ingredients

1Lb (450g) liver.
1Lb (450g) self raising flour.
Old bread crusts etc if you have them
4 eggs.
1 cloves of garlic.
water.

Method

Blitz the liver and garlic in a food processor.
Add the eggs and blend to a sponge mixture
Add water if required

Empty contents into a baking tray.
Bake at 180 degrees for 35 - 45 minutes.

Allow to cool.

Divide into pieces and freeze in small bags ready to take out when training or even showing

p.s. Liver fed "neat" either raw or cooked tends to be too rich for most Irish Wolfhounds, the same applies to heart. It may cause vomiting or scouring.

CHAPTER 7

Grooming

Like many things, grooming your Wolfhound is best started when the dog is a young puppy so that he becomes familiar with being groomed, handled and also having parts of the body checked such as ears, eyes, mouth and feet. In the early days, a puppy coat does not require much maintenance, but the effort put in at this stage will pay dividends later on. We would recommend a light grooming with a soft brush or comb a few times a week and also check inside the dog's ears and mouth and ensure the puppy becomes very accustomed to having its paws checked and any dirt and debris gently removed.

For the first few months, a puppy's coat is quite easy to deal with and very fluffy and soft, but this puppy fur will gradually come out, and the adult coat will grow through and will be harsher in texture and require more maintenance. There is quite a variety of coat textures and types in Wolfhound adults, some dogs have easier maintenance coats which are lighter in density and not as harsh to the touch, but other Wolfhounds will develop a very dense, thick, coarse coat that demands more grooming and maintenance for it to remain in good condition. Grooming is important for any breed of dog. Regular coat maintenance cannot only keep the dog looking in good condition, but it can also help to identify any potential 'undesirables' on the dog's skin or in the fur, highlighting health problems. Owners need to be familiar with their own Wolfhound's coat type and what should and shouldn't be lurking underneath it.

Tools

It is not necessary to buy a raft of expensive grooming tools, you just require some basic brushes and combs, and then the rest is down to personal preference. An essential Wolfhound Grooming kit should contain a dog comb of some description, a brush suitable for the individual's coat, a stripping knife, and some nail clippers. Also, some method for cleaning inside the dog's ears is essential, either a moistened cotton wool, ear wipes or a proprietary ear cleaner.

A comb can be used all over the dog's body and needs to be big enough to go over the general body, but small enough to do finer areas such as the Wolfhound's feet and legs. Many dog combs now have two different sides with differing prongs – prongs that are wider apart will take out any large pieces of dirt and debris and prongs closer together or of different lengths are better for removing smaller particles, undercoat and any mats in the fur.

There is a bewildering variety of dog brushes on the market, and it can be confusing when deciding which brush is right for the job, mostly you need a brush to remove any dirt and debris and a brush to remove dead undercoat. A pin headed brush is an excellent all purpose tool and will remove most items from the coat and is not harsh on a dog or puppy's skin. Many pin head brushes are cushioned at the base of the pins and have the bonus of a bristle brush on the other side:

Removing undercoat from a Wolfhound can be daunting, especially if the dog is densely coated and easily becomes matted. The dead undercoat must be removed to allow the coat to regenerate and also maintain air circulation near the skin. Again there are plenty of tools to choose from for this grooming, but over the years we have found that the multiple blade de-shedders are the most efficient and recommend favourite brands such as the Mars Coat King. However, ensure that the number of blades and size of the tool is appropriate – a 10 or 12 blade tool is excellent for general undercoat removal on the body, but a 16 or 18 blade version is better for finer areas or if the dog is not densely coated. If you only want to purchase one blade de-shedder then go for the 16 or 18 blade version as this will also do the same thing as a 10 or 12 blade, but will just take a bit longer.

Some of these tools are available in a double width, which makes grooming an adult Wolfhound a lot quicker, but please bear in mind that these items have blades on the end and they are sharp – watch your fingers and be careful on delicate/bony areas. We would not recommend using these tools on the head, face, ears, legs, feet or the dog's underside.

Regularly checked your Wolfhound's feet and remove excess fur around the edge of the foot and the bottom of the foot with a stripping knife or round-edged scissors. The fur on the underside of the feet and in between the pads should only be trimmed to make the fur level with the surface of the foot and parting the pads to trim deep inside the foot must be avoided. Nails will need to be checked and trimmed regularly and again this is something that is better started with a puppy, rather than leaving it until later in life. Regular small amounts of trimming on a dog's claws are much better and easier than having to remove significant amounts of nail growth. There is a nerve inside the nail and the nail bed will bleed profusely if accidentally caught, but by regularly trimming the tips of the nails back, the 'quick' as it is known, will recede. A decent pair of guillotine style or pliers style nail clippers will do the job and are relatively inexpensive.

Wolfhound ears can easily become dirty with mud or other debris and so checking them weekly is a good habit to get into, or if you notice that the dog is scratching its ears. Carefully folding back the ear flap so that the inside of the ear is visible and then gently clean with cotton wool, ear wipe or using a general purpose liquid ear cleaner. Never be tempted to use anything sharp or pointed like a cotton bud as you can easily damage the delicate inner ear and never use powders in the ear canal or anything else that will block the ear's mechanism (unless directed to do so by a vet).

Generally speaking, Wolfhounds do not have difficult coats to maintain, but as with many things, regular checking and grooming will keep your dog in optimum condition. It is also a good idea to find a recommended professional dog groomer in your area, as they can be extremely helpful in regular coat care, especially if you are not confident with using some of the grooming tools. There is nothing better than a groomer demonstrating best practice methods for you to then practice at home. Hand stripping a Wolfhound coat is also something that is either best left to a professional groomer or at least ask a groomer to teach you how to do it properly, to avoid any discomfort for the dog and to avoid over-stripping areas of the body.

CHAPTER 8

Parasites

We have a very strict worming protocol, and your puppy was wormed with Panacur 10% at two weeks, 5 weeks, and approximately every 4 weeks after that. Taking into consideration the shunt test, vaccinations dates, etc.

We use Panacur 10%. It is one the most effective wormers for a variety of worms including Giardia. Your puppy will have been wormed with Panacur 10% from being ten to 14 days old and will have been wormed at least three times before they leave for their new homes.

Panacur 10% is a liquid, draw up the recommended dose for the size of the dog in a syringe (no needle attached), the hound's head slightly raised and the mouth slightly open, gently syringe the liquid as far to the back of the mouth as you can, then keep the mouth closed. Alternatively, you can add the dose to food and stir in. If you are administering pills, first coat ours in coconut oil. With one hand hold mouth open, drop coated pill into the mouth, as far back as you can, push down with fingers, at the back of the tongue, tilt head back and hold the mouth closed, at the same time stroking the throat in a downwards action. Rubbing the nose can help if they are breathing excessively through their nose so as not to swallow. Always keep an eye out for pill being spat out!

WE WOULD SUGGEST YOU WORM EVERY 3 MONTHS.

There are four different types of worms: tapeworms, roundworms, hookworms, lungworms. Your dog will display different symptoms depending on what type of worm infection he has, so it's important to recognise the signs.

EXTERNAL PARASITES

At some point in their lives, your pet may come into contact with external "visitors" such as fleas, ticks, or mites.

These parasites will cause scratching and irritation, causing skin problems or carry disease. Treatment, control, and prevention of many external parasites are very simple and please follow your vet's suggestions.

One of the main reasons why it is important to be able to groom your dog is you can check for visitors. Don't just run a brush down their back or along their sides, but lay them down on their side and check underneath too. The soft underbelly is a good place to check for any inflamed areas. Remember to check ears too, and use Cleanaural or Otodene for general maintenance, as they do not contain any antibiotic or steroids. A wipe out with a moist Tea Tree wipe, for a quick refresh. Do not use powders in the ear as it will block forming a plug and make any ear condition worse.

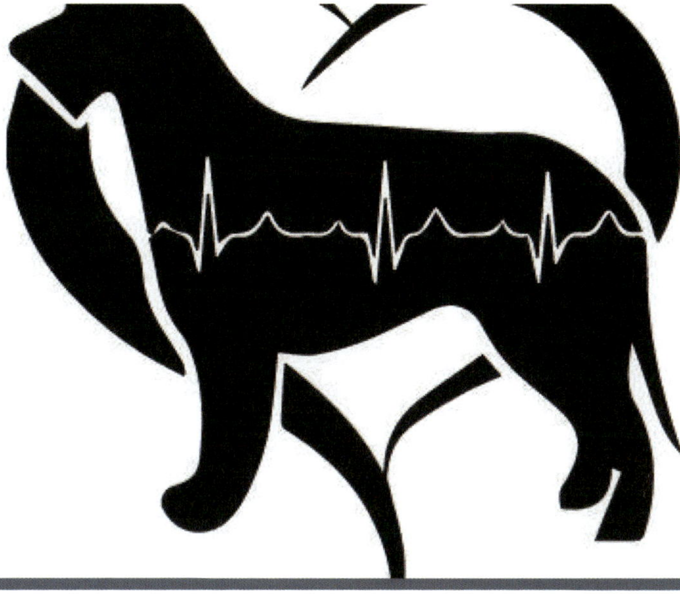

CHAPTER 9

Heart Testing

Heart disease in Irish Wolfhounds has been the subject of research in the UK since 1986. Because it is such a problem, it is recommended that you heart test your Wolfhound every year, you will not only be helping your hound but also contributing to the breed you love.

Heart Testing especially applies to anyone who is breeding. It is by no means a guarantee of heart health, but what it does mean is the breeder is being responsible and taking every precaution possible to use a heart healthy Wolfhound at the time of breeding. It is vital, as cardiovascular disease in Wolfhounds is considered hereditary; there is a 50% chance that a puppy will be affected if the parents are diseased.

We address the issue in the Bonaforte Kennel by heart testing every six months; we are committed to the taking the breed forward with healthy hearts. With this in mind, we decided to go one step further and offer all our owners the opportunity to heart test at the kennel free of charge. This scheme begins when your hound is 18 months to two years old and then annually at Dr Serene Brownlie's (Veterinary Cardiologist) discretion after that so that any dog born here will have an ongoing record of cardiac health.

We have given full permission for all of the results from both our dogs and any of the dogs we have bred, to be entered onto the heart testing database and the findings to be published or be used for further research as Dr Serene Brownlie sees fit.

These are fascinating times, and we feel that the tide is turning regarding health testing in general and a desire to move things forward. We are very excited at the prospect of achieving an accurate picture of the health of our dogs, even though there may be some unpleasant surprises along the way, but when those do crop up, we will take them as a learning opportunity, share our findings, and continue forward with help and support.

Established and well-respected breeders should heart test their Wolfhounds at least once a year. Please always ask to see up to date heart certificates.

A HEALTHY HEART IS A GOOD STARTING POINT.

CHAPTER 10

Upper Respiratory Infections

Kennel Cough does the rounds most years, and Wolfhounds hounds don’t do too well with this virus /bacteria when it does.

An upper respiratory infection, the condition is also known as tracheobronchitis and affects the lungs, windpipe and voice box. It is highly contagious.

Some of the signs can be, coughing up frothy liquid, coughing, high temperature, loss of appetite, dehydration, general unwell appearance, and standing with their neck extended and hanging low.

The thermometer is your best friend here checking for temperature spikes. Oralade is great to have in the cupboard for rehydration, and coconut oils soothe the throat if a cough appears.

The vet is your first port of call, do not wait. You will need antibiotics and maybe rehydration. Acting quickly against this is the best option, when caught in the early stages the recovery is excellent.

As an owner, it is important to be aware of the vital if not subtle signs of the onset of pneumonia, the sooner it is recognised, the better the chance our deep chested hounds have a full recovery.

Once an infection develops deep in the lung tissue, it becomes tough to control, even with the right medication.

The slightest concern or suspicion that your hound may have pneumonia or Kennel Cough above anything else take your wolfhound to the vets. Respiratory problems need to be caught early and quickly before infection takes hold in the lungs.

A WOLFHOUND WILL NORMALLY ADOPT A CERTAIN POSE IF THEY ARE UNWELL. THEY WILL SLOUCH A LITTLE, WITH THEIR NECK EXTENDED IN A DOWNWARD SLOPE, THEIR EYES ARE DULL, EARS MOTIONLESS, AND MOUTH SLIGHTLY OPEN. BREATHING WILL BE LABOURED.

CHAPTER 11

My Wolfhound is Limping

If lameness occurs, you will need to assess it. Firstly check paws and nails, and if the limp is weight bearing with no visible injury, exposed bone or bleeding, apply heat or cold accordingly and "Box Rest." If there is no improvement after 12 to 24hrs, or sooner if your hound is in obvious pain or discomfort, seek veterinary help immediately. If you are in any doubt, then I suggest you seek veterinary help.

If your dog is unable to get up or walk, and or appears in significant discomfort or cannot bear any weight at all on the limb, then your hound requires emergency attention.

“Box Rest”, is my mantra, and it is what I will always say to you when you tell me your puppy or adult hound is limping.

If you are a horsey person, you will know what is meant by this term. The minute a horse is lame, they are stabled on "Box Rest" until sound (not limping), with controlled movement, and gentle short walks if possible. Box rest can be anything from a few days to weeks and sometimes months, depending on the cause and condition.

This same approach must be adopted immediately your Wolfhound starts to limp. Box rest, becomes crate rest, or space where movement is limited, but hound is comfortable. No jumping on and off sofas, or into cars (apart from a trip to the vet), no jumping up, no running around the garden or going on walks.

Box rest, meaning that you never exercise a limping dog. Lame dogs must be allowed to rest completely for a few days to several weeks. When the lameness subsides, continue rest and restrict for another 24-48 hours. Reintroduce moderate exercise such as controlled walks after this period.

If your vet prescribes an anti-inflammatory, firstly use the exact dose you have been instructed to, and secondly, your hound remains on Box Rest! Exercising when taking an anti-inflammatory or pain killer, can worsen the condition when the medication wears off.

If your hound for whatever reason is prescribed an anti-inflammatory (Non-Steroidal Anti-Inflammatory Drugs (NSAIDs) i.e., Rimadyl, Metacam, Deramaxx or Previcox), on a long-term basis, speak with your vet about using it in conjunction with a gastro-protector, such as Omeprazole (Prilosec®, Gastrogard®).

In the last few years, we have heard of several hounds dying from peritonitis following the development of a duodenal ulcer and perforation.

Sadly this was confirmed by Nottingham University, they were sure that NSAIDs were the cause. This condition is tough to pick up on even for the most experienced.

Use NSAIDs, as per instructions, use with care, and give with food, and a gastro-protector if you are looking at long term use.

Another excellent reason to "Box Rest" to avoid overuse of the anti-inflammatory medication, to promote healing by resting.

CHAPTER 12

Umbilical Hernia

An umbilical hernia is when the muscle wall of abdomen doesn't close, and a small bubble-like protrusion under the skin can be seen and felt, as a soft lump on the tummy. Some may extend into the diaphragm.

Most soft hernias will just seal off as the puppy grows, and again we take all hernias under advisement from the vet and is noted on the vaccination card. However, if the vet says an operation will be required, this procedure should be undertaken by the breeder before the puppy leaves for their new home, and the vet is satisfied.

Most umbilical hernias in dogs are inherited, although trauma at birth can also be the cause. I always know if I'm going to end up with a hernia pup through trauma, and despite being mindful of this when whelping, other issues can take priority at the time. Hernias which extend into the diaphragm are more severe and inherited.

However I am also of the opinion that Irish Wolfhounds have more detrimental inherited health issues to be concerned about than umbilical hernias, but if we ever had a very high percentage of hernias from a litter, I would take precautionary steps to prevent this.

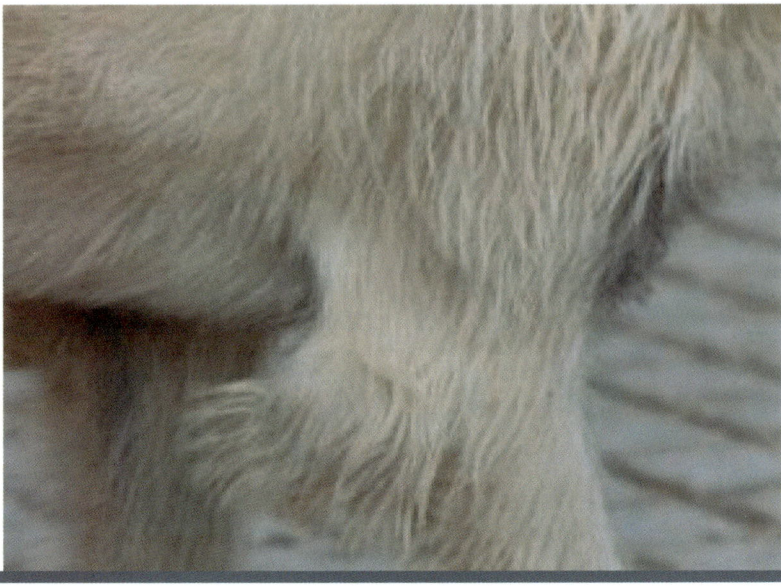

CHAPTER 13

Bursa

Q. My Irish Wolfhound has a swelling on the elbow. What is it?

1. **This is known as a bursa** (Hygromas).

These swellings are filled with fluid, occurring over a bony area, such as the elbow, hocks the top of the head and boney bottoms. They will disappear almost as suddenly as they have appeared off their accord. Irish Wolfhound Bursas are swellings, which can occur on the bony parts, such as elbows, hocks, and bony bottoms. There can start as a small squishy lump and grow. They seem to grow quickly and disappear slowly!

Unless they become infected, hard, extremely large, or causing the dog pain, or lameness, do not drain or otherwise interfered with the bursa. Rather annoyingly they can hang around for several months although they usually disperse given enough time.

Anecdotally success may be achieved by treating bursas, on elbows and bottoms, with homoeopathic Calc Fluor 6c. Some use it in conjunction with Apis Mel 6c. Sometimes the response is good and can be within two weeks of starting treatment.

Dosage: two tablets every two hours for six doses. Next two days- two tablets morning and evening. After that two tablets once a day.

Some owners say they have had a success rate by rubbing haemorrhoid cream on the Bursa!

Some vets will almost certainly suggest draining the bursa and then fill with antibiotics or an anti-inflammatory. Some surgically removed the sac and stitch. My experience is that the bursas will just fill back up again and I avoid this where possible.

Prevention is better than cure. Ensure that your hound has a soft bed to lie/sleep on. However, despite this precautionary measure, dogs can still get bursas. They flop down onto hard surfaces no matter what you try to do to prevent it, preferring the cold tiles of the kitchen floor! Some breed lines seem to have a predisposition and could be because they have the same shape and bony areas or they have the same personality in the way they throw themselves around and flop to the ground. Without a doubt, they are trauma related.

Have some patience, and unless your hound is in pain, these annoying swellings, which seem to appear in an instant, will disappear slowly in their own time. Sometimes they just burst, which is not as bad as it sounds, and this allows the release of the fluid, bathe the area in warm salt water, or in a warm diluted hibiscrub solution, in other words, very keep clean. At this stage it is best you visit your vet, as you may need antibiotics, and your vet may want to put in a few stitches, it is normal they will leave the lower part open so drainage can take place. Unless the bursa bursts or becomes infected, it is best to treat conservatively and not invasively. However always check with your vet if you are unsure.

CHAPTER 14

Sterilisation

Suprelorin is a chemical castration for male dogs rendering them temporarily infertile. The implant lowers testosterone levels, reduces the size of the testes, and decreases libido and decreases the sperm count. The implant takes about year to wear off. It's steroid based - so your dog may just urinate more at first, but this normalises after a few days. Suprelorin will work reasonably quickly and like castration, it may change the energy/personality of your hound and may lead to weight gain.

With the onset of puberty, your hound may appear to change with the increased testosterone levels. With a male hound is it essential that you focus on obedience training them right from the word go. Early training is advantageous when puberty starts, as you can gain your hound's focus keeping them under control.

We use and recommend the implant, instead of castration, but please don't go down this route of either form of castration until your hound has fully grown. We suggest at least over the age of two; it will vary but never please younger than this.

Please ask your vet about Suprelorin as an alternative to castration as is does avoid the need for an anaesthetic.

A male Wolfhound can be, shall we say, a bit more challenging when his testosterone kicks in, and this is one of the reasons why for individual families and first-time Wolfhound owners we always recommend having a girl.

Bitches, I prefer not to spay. Although there are female implants, I have never used them but know that other owners are pleased with the results, especially if a bitch is not healthy enough to have surgery. The worry as always with the Wolfhounds is the anaesthetic.

Many vets and breeders alike still believe that early sterilisation effects growth. Some vets, however, will perform the procedure very young. My opinion at the moment is if you are going to carry this out then wait until the hound has fully grown, so you are looking at 24 to 30 months of age.

Please discuss this procedure with your vet.

CHAPTER 15

Hidden Testicle

The testicles start off in the abdomen just behind the kidneys, and during gestation and with the help of male hormones they enter the inguinal (groin) region shortly after birth.

Normally the testicles drop into the scrotum anywhere between 10 and 40 days. However, it 's hard to confirm this has happened, as they are tiny and soft. Our vet at the 8-week health examination checks if the testes are in place as a matter of course.

If they are not in place the vet makes a note of this on the vaccination card, this reminds us to keep checking and keeps our owners informed; it also acts as a reminder for your vet to re-check. There is always a chance that between 2 and 6 months the already descended testes may retract, this can be in response to a muscle (cremaster muscle) contracting in response to cold, stress or fear.

Between the abdomen and the scrotum there is an area, which closes off at around 6 months, and when this happens, the testes are blocked from dropping down. In giant breeds, it can take longer to close, and an undescended testicle may drop up to 12 months later.

When one or both testes do not descend by 12 months, this is called an ectopic testis or cryptorchidism (meaning hidden testicle). It is more common for one testicle to be undescended than both, this could be a genetic disorder and performing this mating again isn't advisable. Please discuss the outcome with your vet, as it may or may not have health implications depending on the research of the day.

CHAPTER 16

Pica

Pica is a term used for having an appetite for things that have no nutritional value, for example, paper, stones, wood, clothes, pebbles, cables, etc. Some of these items can be harmful, toxic and or cause obstructions, constipation or damage to the intestines.

Certain breeds are more prone than others, but puppies of all breeds tend to experience pica. There could be medical reasons and deficiencies in the diet for pica, but generally, it is a behavioural issue.

If you experience this with your puppy or dog, the first route is to distract them. Lack of exercise, boredom, stress or anxiety may be contributing reasons. Please check with your vet to ensure there isn't a medical reason, but a bored Wolfhound who feels they aren't getting enough attention, enough toys or fun things to do, will devise a million and one ways to ensure they do and pica is one of them.

PS. Dogs do eat grass, and it is not necessarily a sign that they are poorly, and they won't always sick it up, the undigested grass does pass through and is seen in the poo!

CHAPTER 13

Check List

- Do not let puppy out of the car on the way home he may not be fully vaccinated
- Please do not let puppy jump in and out of your car, always assist to reduce impact.
- Puppy maybe a little upset for the first few days but this will soon settle especially with lots of love and cuddles
- Do not leave puppy unattended at anytime with older dogs, no matter how placid.
- Puppy will need a safe place to rest and sleep for the first year

- A separate bed where they can't get into mischief or a large crate

- Do not give puppy soft stuff toys, your hound will rip them to shreds and may then swallow. This can lead to horrendous problems & blockages.

- Puppy will be eating 4 meals a day to start with
- Feed Puppy one scoop per meal: a mix of Bonaforte's (80%) and Bonaforte's Salmon & Trout. (20%)
- Puppy has been eating this dry. Plus 20ml Olive Oil per day.

- Increasing food as puppy eats the bowl clean each time.

- Meals can be taken to 3 times per day as puppy grows.

- Ribs should be felt but not seen.

- Do not feed puppy human food (they have all their nutritional requirements in the kibble) until settled into their new home, as this may cause tummy upsets.

- Always have plenty of clean fresh water available. Stainless bowels are practical and more hygienic.

- Do not exercise Puppy or a fully grown hound on a full tummy.

- Leave approximately one/two hours after eating before exercising.

- Puppy may have had the first vaccine, but may require a second: see card inside puppy pack.

- Do not do a re-start with the vaccines.

- Puppy has been vet checked. See vaccination card for any issues found.

- Puppy is insured for 4 weeks. Please carry on with insurance for at least the first year.

- Puppy has been micro-chipped. Please register your contact details.

- Please do not overfeed your hound

- Collar and Lead - It is now law that all dogs must wear a collar in public places and must have an tag attached with your details.

- You are also required to carry poo bags for collecting poo when you are in a public place.

- Supervised exercise only

CHAPTER 18

Assured Breeder Information

The Kennel Club requires every Assured Breeder to give to new puppy owners the following information.

SOCIALISATION ADVICE

Socialisation is a term that is often used in dog training books, in dog magazines and by breeders and trainers. But what does it actually mean and how will it affect you as a new puppy owner?

Like human children, puppies are not born with the social skills that they require to live with their family, be that a canine family or a human one. The term "socialisation" in simple terms means the learning process that a puppy must undergo in order to learn key life skills to ensure that it is happy and confident in its environment, and can communicate effectively within its social group. We ask a huge amount from our dogs in their role as a companion animal, as not only do they need to understand humans and the human world, they also need to become fluent in the language of dog.

This involves having pleasant social interactions with adults, children, vets, adult dogs and other animals, as well as careful exposure to different situations in the environment like traffic, crowds, travelling in the car, vacuum cleaners and any sights and sounds it will have to cope with in life. It is so important that this is done thoroughly and correctly when your puppy is still young and he is young enough to happily accept new things.

Puppies that have been socialised effectively in these early weeks are far less likely to react negatively to new situations, noises, people, dogs and animals than their counterparts, who have not had these important early experiences. A well socialised puppy is far more likely to integrate easily into your life, therefore making your life together much more enjoyable and rewarding.

There are two parts to socialisation and both are equally important. The first is teaching the puppy to be social with people and other dogs, while the other (called habituation) is about teaching all the things we want the puppy to ignore and not be worried about (noises, traffic, household objects etc.).

Being a companion is the hardest job we ever ask a dog to do as our expectations are so high. We want dogs to get on with everybody and everything, and to go everywhere with us when we want, but be happy to be left alone without complaint when we don't, to be accepting of loud noises, strangers, other dogs... The list is endless. It is a sad fact that one of the major causes of death in dogs under two years old is euthanasia, as a result of behaviour problems. Most of these behaviour problems arise from fear (fear of strange noises, fear of being left alone – and indeed aggression nearly always arises from fear – fear of strange dogs, fear of strange people or fear of strange situations). In addition, far too many dogs are ending up in rescue centres. Behaviourists and trainers up and down the country are seeing dogs with problems that could so easily have been prevented if the first 16 weeks of that dog's life had been properly managed, and they had been prepared for the life they were going to lead.

Some breeds need far more socialisation and habituation than others – with more reactive breeds (such as those bred to guard, some terriers etc.) needing more – and earlier – socialisation than others. Therefore, it is important for breeders and new owners to know how reactive their chosen breed is so they can focus their socialisation accordingly.

On the breeders' part, socialising their litter can start as early as when the puppies are a few days old. Gentle handling and checking the progress of the litter are all important steps in the first few days of a puppy's life. Over the course of the following weeks the breeder can introduce noises, different surfaces, different play items as well as different play and feeding locations around the house – all of this habituation and novelty contributes to the puppies' early development. The early ground work that the breeder puts into their litters' social and emotional wellbeing has a direct impact on their puppies' ability to be fit for function as a family dog.

It is imperative that the puppy's new owner continues this when their new puppy comes home. From around 5 weeks and continuing at the time the puppy goes to his or her new home, an important transition takes place in the puppy's ability to take in new situations as his natural fearfulness increases.

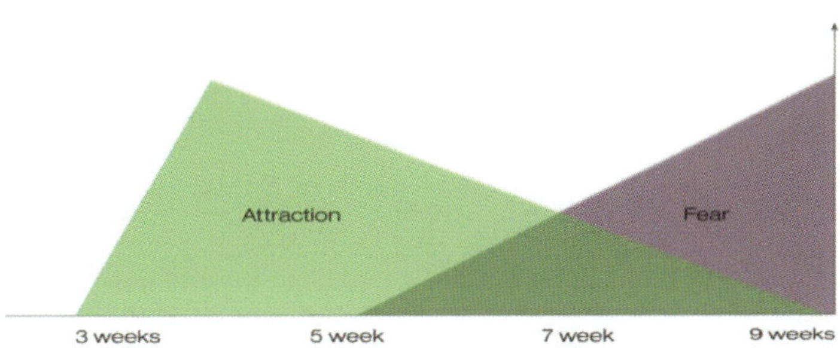

It is therefore so important that new owners don't miss this valuable window of opportunity for their puppy to experience new things – which will close at around 14-16 weeks. This time also coincides with the puppy's vaccinations, so a balance must be struck so not to miss out on this important learning opportunity. This can be achieved by taking your puppy out and about in your arms, while not allowing them to come into direct contact with other dogs until their vaccinations have taken place. Getting out and about with your puppy is key to them accepting everyday things, such as traffic and busy places, as part of normal life. It is important that you think about what life as part of your family will entail for a puppy – for instance, if you live in the inner city spending a significant amount of time socialising your puppy to farm animals may not be of great benefit, as it is unlikely they will encounter them in their day to day life:

Rural Lifestyle	City Lifestyle
Farm animals	Heavy traffic
Farm machinery	Crowds of people
Horses with/without riders	Emergency sirens
Road walking	Public transport

The same also goes for all the different people your puppy is likely to meet such as: people with beards, people wearing hats, people wearing high visibility clothing, babies, children, people with pushchairs/prams, elderly people, people with walking sticks and people in wheelchairs to name but a few, or anyone else you are likely to meet.

Your Bonaforte puppy has experienced the following:

Early Neurological Stimulation

10 different surfaces, but not wooden floors as these can be very slippery.

Radio 2

Washing machine noise, dishwasher noise, feed bowls being clattered, plastic bags, general kitchen noise, light traffic noise

Been handled by at least 8 people by 4 weeks + a journey by car to the vets - and further handling.

Puppy parties

Vet surgeries often hold 'puppy parties' for their new clients, but these should be treated with some caution. Well managed puppy parties can be great social interaction for puppies of all ages and sizes. Well managed parties should:

- Match puppies up according to their size so that the bolder puppies don't intimidate the more nervous or smaller ones, and thereby create negative experiences for the smaller puppies, and make the bolder ones 'social bullies'.
- Manage any off-lead play carefully and if necessary, separate puppies that get a bit too boisterous so that they can calm down and re-join the party once they are calmer.
- Discourage any kind of anti-social behaviour, such as biting that gets out of hand, very rough play and also show the owners how to discourage this.
- Show owners how to handle and groom their puppies – and have others do this too.
- Be fun positive experiences for puppies and owners.

The Puppy Socialisation Plan

Until now there was no definitive plan for effectively socialising your puppy, which was resulting in rescue centres seeing increasing numbers of dogs coming to them with behavioural issues that could have been avoided with proper socialisation. In order to counteract this, the Kennel Club and Dogs Trust have jointly devised a socialisation plan for both breeders and new owners to follow as a step by step guide - it is called the Puppy Socialisation Plan. Both the Kennel Club and Dogs Trust recommend the Puppy Socialisation Plan as an effective plan for breeders and new owners to prepare their puppies as best they can for life as family pets. It is simple to complete, and can be tailored to suit you and your lifestyle, so it is highly recommended that novice breeders and new owners follow the Plan.

It is critical that this is done from birth up to 16 weeks of age, otherwise important learning and development phases have passed. The Plan covers everything from getting used to household noises, to getting out and about and meeting new people and other dogs. Therefore, you need to plan and incorporate some extremely important life lessons during the early stages of your puppy's development, so that you end up with a well-balanced and sociable dog.□ □

You can find The Puppy Socialisation Plan located at - http://www.thepuppyplan.com/

EXERCISE ADVICE

An important part of a dog's life is exercise, not only for fitness, but also for mental stimulation. Indeed exercise times and feeding times are often the most exciting parts of a dog's day, and your puppy will grow to keenly anticipate them.

Small beginnings

Puppies need much less exercise than fully-grown dogs. If you over-exercise a growing puppy, you can quickly overtire it, and more importantly damage its developing joints, which may cause early arthritis. A good rule of thumb is a ratio of five minutes exercise per month of age (up to twice a day), until the puppy is fully grown, i.e. 15 minutes when three months old, 20 minutes when four months old etc. See the Bonaforte website for breed-specific exercise information relating to your puppy.

Exercise Requirements

- **0-12 weeks. Until a puppy has completed its course of vaccinations, there is a risk of infection. Therefore, it is usually**

better that exercise is restricted to within the confines of your garden. Exercise in the garden also provides an excellent opportunity to start early training, and to get your puppy used to wearing a collar. Make sure your puppy has a number of safe toys, and always accompany them in the garden. This way, you can engage your puppy in suitable levels of activity, and start to reward good toileting behaviour, which can usually provide all the puppy's exercise needs during this time. If the opportunity arises, take your puppy to other safe environments where there is no risk, and it is able to mix with other animals and people, such as private gardens where only vaccinated dogs have access. Socialising at an early age is a vital part of your dog's development.

It is important that puppies and dogs go out for exercise every day in a safe and secure area, or they may become frustrated. Time spent in the garden (however large) is no substitute for exploring new environments, and socialising with other dogs. When you go out, make sure your puppy is trained to recall, so that you are confident the puppy will return to you when called (see the accompanying sheet on 'Training your Puppy').

You should never exercise your puppy on a full stomach as this may contribute to bloat or stomach dilation which can sometimes prove fatal.

All dogs require regular exercise to remain fit and prevent them from becoming overweight, which may also lead to health problems. You should remember however, that exercise needs to be introduced gradually, and that a young puppy will not have the same exercise requirement as an adult dog.

The duration and frequency of exercise should remain consistent and any increases should be gradual. For the majority of dogs, exercise is an important part of their life and so they will take as much as you can give. A dog will also enjoy play, whether with you or on its own, and so toys play an important part in a dog's life.

Dependant on breed and temperament and mobility, a dog will normally be capable of walking to the same capability as its owner, however as a dog becomes older, exercise should be reduced and your dog should be allowed to walk at its own pace.

PUPPY TRAINING ADVICE

Bringing your puppy home for the first time is naturally a happy and exciting occasion, but it can be a little daunting too – there is so much for both you and your puppy to learn! The information below should help you on your way to raising a happy and well trained dog right from the start.

Important training tips:
Start as you mean to go on. If you are always consistent you will avoid confusing your puppy. Puppies have a very short attention span so train for short spells on a regular basis
Keep it short and keep it simple, but most of all keep it fun. Puppies respond better to cheerful voice tones rather than to threatening orders. Gentle play builds trust and a strong bond between you and your puppy as well as making training fun. Patience is the KEY ingredient in dog training. If you try to rush things you will only get frustrated and confuse your puppy. Keep it interesting: cultivate a range of different rewards incorporating play, fuss, praise, treats and toys. This will stop both of you from getting bored.

Toilet training puppies the easy way
Toilet training is obviously a crucial part of your puppy's early learning. Getting it right is relatively simple, and will make those first weeks so much more enjoyable for you both. However, like all things, bad habits learnt early on can lead to problems that may take weeks or even months to resolve.

Initially, you will have to build your daily routine around your puppy's needs. Fortunately, these are quite predictable when they are very young, and with careful supervision you should quickly establish when it is the right time to go outside and minimise any accidents.

Like babies, puppies have poor bladder control, and need to go to the toilet several times an hour when they are awake. They will also usually need to be taken outside first thing in the morning, last thing at night, after each meal, waking from a nap, and after any exercise, play or excitement. You may find it useful to keep a record of when your puppy sleeps, eats and goes to the toilet so that you can identify any patterns that emerge. One tip is to use a food timer to remind you when it is time to take your puppy outside to relieve itself. If you find that your puppy needs to "go" every 20 minutes then set the alarm as soon as he has gone and take him outside the moment the alarm goes off.

Always go with your puppy into the garden and establish a regular spot. Puppies are creatures of habit, so as long as you introduce the garden to the puppy as its toilet area early on, you should be able to avoid most accidents. Decide on a cue word or phrase to use when the puppy is actually going to the toilet, so that the puppy will start to associate the word with the action and should learn to go on command. By accompanying your puppy into the garden each time, you will be there to attach cue words and praise to any successful actions.

If toilet training is not going quite as well as planned, some common reasons for why your puppy is struggling are as follows:

Feeding

- You are feeding the puppy too much.
- The puppy food you are giving is unsuitable or you are giving too much variety for a puppy of their age.
- You are not feeding at regular times.
- You are feeding at the wrong times (which could mean your puppy needs to go to the toilet during the night).
- You are giving foods which are too salty, causing your puppy to drink more.

Training

Punishing your puppy for accidents indoors may make it scared of going to the toilet in front of you – even outside. Expecting your puppy to tell you when it needs to go to the toilet is unrealistic. It is far better to go outside at regular intervals. Leaving the back door or outside access open for your puppy to come and go as it pleases can cause confusion – particularly when that access is closed. Do not leave your puppy too long on its own so that it is forced to go indoors. Leaving your puppy alone in the garden means that you are not there to praise and reward, or to reinforce the idea that the garden is the correct place to go. Try to avoid using the words "good boy/girl" when your puppy is going to the toilet - you don't want your puppy going to the toilet every time it is praised. Puppies can exhibit submissive or excitable urination when greeting you on your return home. Toning down greetings can help prevent your puppy from becoming overexcited. Young puppies will not be able to go through the night without needing to go to the toilet. If they do wake you up, it really is worth getting up to let them out.

Environment

Being surrounded by lots of absorbent or grass-like surfaces, such as rugs and carpets, may confuse your puppy. Ammonia based cleaning products used around the house can smell like urine to your puppy, and lead to unwanted accidents. If your puppy does have an accident inside, the scent will still be apparent to the puppy for a long time afterwards, even if you have thoroughly disinfected the area. Specialist cleaning products specifically designed to mask the odour are available.

Beyond the garden, many owners can be disappointed that their young puppy does not initially toilet when first venturing out on walks. Often, your puppy will only relieve itself the second you get home. This is because the puppy has not yet associated going out for a walk as an opportunity to go to the toilet, so will wait until they return home to their garden, which they know is a good place to go.

To break this habit, get up a little earlier in the morning (when you have plenty of time) and take your puppy out on a walk before it has had a chance to visit its usual spot. Stay out with your puppy for a reasonable length of time until it has been to the toilet, and then give plenty of praise. If you are not successful, make sure the puppy is whisked into the garden to relieve itself or you will run the risk of a large puddle indoors!

Remember, patience and consistency is key. All puppies take different amounts of time to learn, so don't worry if your puppy seems to be taking longer to get the hang of things. Your patience will pay off and you will both get there in the end.

A trained dog is a happy dog
Housetraining aside, every puppy also needs to be taught good manners and have constructive lessons in basic control and social interaction. This includes:

- Responding to its name.
- Learning how to greet and behave politely around other people and dogs.
- To come back when called.
- To walk nicely on the lead.
- To sit down and stay on command.
- To allow itself to be groomed and examined by you and your vet.

Dog training classes
Most owners can benefit from attending good training classes, and training in the company of other dogs is very useful, because of the realistic distractions it involves. Ideally, you should start your classes as soon as your puppy's vaccinations are complete, but classes can be invaluable for older dogs too, and continue throughout the dog's life.

There are lots of schools of thought on dog training and it is naturally important that you find a class and training instructors with the right approach for you and your puppy. Dog training can be lots of fun and very rewarding. After all, a trained dog is a happy dog, and a happy dog makes for a happy owner too.

Finding the best dog training club

Before enrolling with a dog training club it can be beneficial to go and visit several classes first (without your puppy) to make sure you have made the right choice. Things you may wish to consider include:

- Do you like what you see – are the trainers friendly, are people happy and enjoying training their dogs?
- Are the dogs happily focused on their human family?
- Are the instructors giving lots of encouragement and information to all attendees?
- Are the instructors maintaining a controlled, safe environment for all?
- Are instructors treating everyone fairly and meeting the needs of the whole group?

You can find training classes by using the Kennel Club's Find a Club service – visit www.findaclub.org.uk to find a club near you running training classes, or call the Kennel Club on 01269 318540. . You can also ask your vet and other dog owners for recommendations.

The Kennel Club Good Citizen Dog Scheme

The Kennel Club Good Citizen Dog Scheme is the UK's largest dog training programme, and has been introduced to assist owners in training their dogs to be obedient in every day situations. Its simple but effective dog training techniques encompass all the skills necessary for a happy and rewarding partnership with your dog. There are four levels of the Scheme, namely Puppy Foundation, Silver, Bronze and Gold. Each level is designed to further develop an owner's understanding of training, while building a dog's confidence and levels of obedience. All dogs are eligible to take part, whether they are young or old, pedigree or crossbreed. Over

2000 dog training schools throughout the UK offer Scheme training courses.

The Kennel Club Accreditation Scheme for Instructors in Dog Training and Canine Behaviour

The Kennel Club Accreditation Scheme for Instructors in Dog Training and Canine Behaviour (KCAI) is the UK's first and only national and verified qualification in dog training and canine behaviour, recognised by City & Guilds. Representing the 'gold standard' in teaching, advice and service, members of the Scheme abide by a strict Code of Practice designed to ensure that dog owners are provided with the best advice and service. Look for the badge of quality when you are choosing a trainer. You can see which clubs have KCAI Accredited instructors on the Kennel Club's Find a Club service.

DIET ADVICE

Feeding your puppy sensibly and correctly is vital to its health, development and general wellbeing. Below you will find details of your puppy's current diet and more information can be found on thewww.Bonaforte.com website.

Little and often

Like all infants, puppies grow very rapidly (up to twenty times faster than an adult dog), and so require a specially formulated diet to aid their physical development. A high energy growth food is recommended and needs to be fed at evenly spaced intervals to avoid over stretching your puppy's small stomach.

Meals should be split during the course of the day and ideally a young puppy should go approximately 4 hours between meals.

It is better not to leave food down (so throw away any uneaten food after 20 minutes) and not to change your puppy's food regularly as this could cause havoc with its digestion and toilet training regime. Make sure that water is always available to your puppy, so never take its water bowl away.

Quantities

The quantity of food should be approximately the same for each meal. Young puppies, particularly those of a large or fast growing breed, can sometimes need more food as puppies than they require as adults. Increases of food should always be gradual and a good idea is to increase the amount on a weekly basis from 8 weeks until the puppy is 16 weeks old. Typically, by the time a puppy reaches 16 weeks, it will need roughly the same amount as when it is an adult.

Puppies can be greedy or picky with their food so it can sometimes be difficult to gauge how much to give them. Care should be taken not to over or underfeed your puppy. Puppies can often appear 'chubby', particularly after they have eaten, but under normal circumstances they should have a defined 'waist'. If in any doubt about your puppy's weight or diet, consult your vet when you next visit for a puppy check-up.

There are many varied feeding regimes to choose from: dry complete diets, semi-moist or pouch, tinned food (with or without biscuit mixer), raw food, and home-made food. Each food category has different qualities, and finding the right balance for your puppy is extremely important.

The most suitable diet should be easily digested and produce dark brown, firm, formed stools. If your puppy produces soft or light stools or has wind or diarrhoea, then the diet may not suit your puppy or it might have some kind of digestive problem or infection. If the condition persists for more than 2 days, consult your vet for advice.

Please remember that stability in the diet will help maintain good digestion. Any change in diet should be made very gradually over at least a week to avoid upset and you should try a new diet for at least 10 days before making any further changes.

Dry complete foods

There is a wide range of dry complete foods on the market and the quality varies widely. To get the best out of your puppy's development choose a food specially designed for puppies. Some puppies are not accustomed to complete dry foods immediately after weaning but will normally grow to like them with time. If your puppy does not seem to like eating dry complete and this is what you wish to feed, you can try soaking the food in a little warm water to soften it, or mix in a tin of sardines gradually reducing the quantity until your puppy is fully weaned and accepts dry complete. See puppy menu on the Bonaforte website for more details.

Semi-moist, pouch, tinned and frozen foods

As with complete dry foods, semi-moist, pouch, tinned and frozen foods can vary in quality. Again, choose a good quality diet which is easily digestible, nutritionally complete and does not require additional foods to be added to it. As before it is best to avoid changes in your puppy's diet - so if you find a product that works for your puppy, stick to it.

Home-made food (raw fresh or frozen meat)

Before the advent of commercial dog foods, it was quite common to feed dogs raw or cooked fresh meat. Many people still consider that there is no substitute for feeding raw meat; these diets are sometimes referred to as BARF (Bones and raw food diet). Meat on its own however, is not enough, and dogs need other ingredients, for example biscuit, and supplements to maintain a completely balanced diet. Puppies in particular, need a balanced and nutritious diet whilst they are growing up, as even a slight imbalance may harm their development and growth. Additionally, home-made foods obviously necessitate a fair degree of pre-planning and preparation. However, there are a number of manufacturers now providing pre-packaged complete BARF diets, which make the feeding regime easier to administer.

Treats

Giving treats is a good way to reward your dog during training and encourage the behaviour you want. There are a wide variety of prepared and natural treats on the market which vary hugely in quality. Some commercial treats have lots of sugar, colourings, milk products and fat in them, so always check the ingredients label. Good quality prepared treats have been developed with dogs dietary needs in mind.

However, all treats should be given sparingly, and never comprise more than 15% of your puppy's total calorie intake. If you use treats regularly, reduce the amount of main meal food your dog is receiving in order to avoid obesity. Some chew treats have proven ability to help prevent dental diseases, but again check the label to ensure you are getting a genuine product.

Human chocolate is poisonous to dogs and can cause liver damage and even be fatal, so never give your dog any chocolate, or leave any lying around where it might be found and eaten. Be especially careful at Christmas and Easter time.

Avoid giving your puppy any sweet biscuits or sugary treats which are bad for its teeth as well as its waistline, and can cause sugar 'highs' and 'lows'. Stick to prepared which tend to be much more popular.

Always remember that table scraps contain calories so they should be taken into account as part of the daily diet. Better still; don't be tempted to feed table scraps at all.

Food sensitivities and intolerances

Like humans, some dogs are sensitive or intolerant to certain foods, and this can cause a variety of problems. In extreme cases, they may develop colitis (slime and blood in their stools). Always consult your vet if you notice you dog displaying any of the following symptoms:

- **Lethargy.**
- **Aggressive or hyperactive behaviour.**
- **Chronic skin and ear problems.**
- **Light to mid-brown loose bulky stools or diarrhoea.**
- **Slime or jelly being passed with stools and flatulence.**
- **Bloating and weight gain or loss.**

Irish Wolfhounds can be very sensitive to dietary changes and additions. Please try and stay with our feeding program.

Feeding tips

- **Clean fresh water should always be available. Dogs eating wet food (i.e. canned) will receive moisture through their food and therefore require less water than dogs eating dry food. However, whatever the diet, water should always be made available.**
- **Do not refill half empty bowls, but ensure that fresh food is always provided at each meal time. This is particularly true in the hot weather when food left in bowls can attract flies and other insects.**
- **Half full cans of dog food should be kept covered in the fridge, but allowed to stand until the food is up to room temperature before feeding.**
- **There are two different types of dog food manufactured "complete" and "complementary", clearly marked on the label. A complete food can be fed as a sole source of nutrition and is available as both canned and dry food. A complementary food**

is designed to accompany the complete food and should not be used as the only source of daily nutrition.

- **It is better to stick to one variety of complete puppy food, so you don't need to add anything to the diet. Always remember that over-supplementing can be harmful to your puppy.**
- **If your puppy does not eat all of its meal in one go, you may be offering it too much. Not all puppies eat the amount recommended by the pet food manufacturers. Puppies' appetites can vary enormously, with some eating much less than the recommended amounts, whilst others scoff their meal down as if it was their last!**
- **As long as your puppy is not showing any growth or digestive problems, resist the temptation to change its diet or offer it a range of foods, as you may turn your puppy into a fussy eater.**
- **Never change your puppy's diet abruptly (unless under the direction of your vet). If you want to change its diet, do it gradually over a period of a few days to a week or longer if necessary.**
- **Avoid feeding your puppy before travelling in the car, as this can encourage car sickness.**
- **Do not feed your puppy an hour before or after exercise or play, as this could lead to stomach dilation and torsion (also known as bloat), which is a life threatening condition requiring immediate veterinary intervention. For owners of breeds which are thought to be susceptible to this condition, you should seek advice from your breeder, vet and/or breed club on further precautionary measures.**
- **Leave your puppy in peace while it is eating from its bowl. Taking the bowl away while it is eating causes anxiety and this can lead to food aggression. If you want to be sure that your puppy is comfortable with you approaching it during mealtimes, add a little food to the bowl while it is eating, so it sees you as an asset, rather than a threat.**
- **Never feed your dog from the table or your plate, as this encourages drooling and attention seeking behaviours, such as begging and barking.**

Potential Toxins/Poisons (this list is by no means complete and always consult your vet if you puppy ingests anything it shouldn't)

- Alcohol.
- Chocolate.
- Coffee/Caffeine.
- **Grapes/Raisins/Currants/Sultanas.**
- **Artificial sweeteners containing xylitol.**
- Some human vitamins and supplements.
- Mouldy food.
- Onions, chives and garlic.
- Slug pellets and other pesticides.
- Yeast/Dough.
- Some garden/household plants.
- Macadamia nuts.
- Brassica plants (cabbage, broccoli, cauliflower, swede, turnip)

Information reviewed by PFMA Veterinary and Nutrition Committee. For more information on poisons please visit www.thekennelclub.org.uk/health/pet-health-information/common-canine-poisons/

Grooming Advice

www.bonaforte.com

for breed grooming tips

All dogs will benefit from regular grooming, whether they are a short haired breed or one with a long or fluffy coat.

Reasons for grooming – Remember 'CHAIR'

Cleanliness – keeping your dog's coat clean by removing dirt and dead hair helps encourage new hair growth, and reduces the amount of hair deposited on household furniture

Health – grooming helps to stimulate new coat growth, and prevents the formation of knots or matting which may lead to skin irritation
Appearance – most owners take a pride in their dogs looking smart, and regular grooming will certainly help your puppy to look its best
Inspection – regular grooming is also a great way to check for parasites, or any suspicious lumps and bumps
Relationship – grooming is part of dog's socialisation activities. Regular grooming helps create a bond between you and your puppy, and accustoms your puppy to being handled. Do remember that grooming should include checking ears, nails, teeth, and eyes etc. on a regular basis.

Getting started

It is important to groom your puppy at a height which is comfortable for both you and your dog. For many dogs it may be advisable to groom them on a table and custom made grooming tables are available. But any sturdy table or work bench with a non-slip surface will suffice. Remember: **never** leave your puppy unattended on the table for even a short moment.

Start the grooming experience at an early age as part of your puppy's socialisation programme and routines. Keep the sessions short to start off with – just a couple of minutes, gradually increasing the time spent on the table. Always make the experience positive, rewarding with praise and suitable treats. Any struggling should be dealt with firmly but kindly, as your puppy may be frustrated, mischievous or even afraid.

Build up the experience and your puppy will come to accept the grooming routine and also being handled on the table. This will help with other activities such as veterinary visits.

Finish the grooming if your puppy shows signs of getting bored or tired, so that each session ends on a positive note.

Dog coat types

It's worth bearing in mind that factors like neutering, age, poor diet and poor health can dramatically influence your dog's coat.

Your Puppy's Grooming Requirements

See notes on the www.bonaforte.com website.

Knots and matts

A knot occurs where the coat is slightly tangled but it can be removed by careful brushing or combing out. Matts are formed when dead, loose undercoat hair becomes trapped by the top or guard hair, and starts to clump and twist together. If this matted coat becomes wet, the matting tightens and becomes almost solid. Do not attempt to remove matts unless trained in the procedure. Otherwise, refer to a professional groomer.

Care of ears, nails and eyes

- Check your puppy's ears to see if they are clean. You can remove excess dirt from the inside of the ear flap with damp cotton wool. Never probe inside the ear as you may perforate the ear drum. Any odour is usually a sign there is something wrong and your puppy should be taken to a vet.
- If nails are excessively long remove the tip of the claw, taking care not to cut the quick or blood vessel.
- If needed clean the eyes with clean, damp cotton wool using a separate piece for each eye.

External Parasites

A parasite is something that lives on another animal (the host) and gets its nourishment from the host. If left unchecked, the parasite causes disease or even death. The most common external parasites found on dogs are fleas and ticks.

- Fleas are very small, brownish black, extremely agile creatures. Excessive scratching and self-biting can be symptoms of flea infestation. Even if no fleas are to be seen the presence of shiny black specks like coal dust (flea excreta) is a sure indication of the presence of fleas (dab the specks with a damp piece of cotton wool and if it goes pink it confirms the presence of fleas; these are the remains of a digested blood meal from the host).

- Ticks are largish grey pea shaped parasites that can be 3 to 4mm in length. They attach themselves to other animals in order to have a blood meal. There is evidence that ticks are also a threat to human health as they can spread Lyme disease.

There is now a wide range of proprietary powders, sprays, 'spot-on' treatments and anti-flea and tick collars available. A dedicated pet care professional will be happy to advise on suitable products.

Other skin problems

- Ringworm is a fungal disease, affecting the skin, nails and hair. Circular lesions appear causing hair loss, which become scaly and crusty. Ringworm is contagious and is a zoonotic condition (transmissible to humans).
- Dermatitis causes irritation, hair loss and inflammation and is a result of sensitivity to the environment.
- Alopecia can range from a thinning of hair to total hair loss and can be caused by a number of factors such as skin parasites, hormonal imbalance, infections, stress or poor nutrition. Seek veterinary advice for any skin problems.

Professional grooming

Some breeds of dog may require professional trimming and styling. Most coated breeds will require full grooming about once every four to six weeks but even short coated breeds can benefit from a 'wash and brush' up more regularly to remove dust and dirt.

WORMING ADVICE

Worming your dog throughout its lifetime is important, and you should talk to your vet about a suitable worming programme for your puppy at the earliest opportunity. Regular worming not only protects your dog's health, but helps to prevent the spread of infection and potentially hazardous health risks to other animals and humans too. Worm infections carried by your dog do not always display obvious symptoms, so an adequate treatment schedule is vital.

Some worming treatment has been carried out prior to you receiving your puppy and a record of this is provided in the chart below. Do discuss this further with your own veterinary surgeon.

Date Wormed	Product Used	Amount Given
2 weeks	Panacur 10%	1m per day over 3 days
4 weeks	Panacur 10%	1m per day over 3 days
8 weeks	MILBEMAX	2x tab dog/pup
Date next treatment due:	Please consult with your vet about your worming plan	

Signs aren't always obvious

Dogs can appear healthy even when they have worm infections. Detecting an infection can be tricky, particularly as worm eggs are too small to be easily visible in your pet's faeces. In addition, your dog may be more at risk from some worm infections than others depending on where you live. It is therefore extremely important to keep your dog's treatment regular and up-to-date.

Specific signs will be described for each worm, but remember that not all worm infections will be obvious in your dog, so some more general signs to look for include:

- **The presence of visible worm segments that could stick to your dog's bottom and become itchy. This can cause dogs to "scoot", whereby they drag their bottoms along the ground with their back legs. Doing this also means that**

your dog will be rubbing its infected bottom on your floor or carpet, which is naturally unhygienic.

- **Weight loss.**
- **Vomiting.**
- **Diarrhoea.**
- **A dull, lifeless coat.**
- **A change in appetite (it may be either increased or decreased depending on the worms present).**
- **A lack of energy.**
- **A pot-bellied appearance (most commonly seen in puppies).**
- **Breathing difficulties and coughing.**

You should seek advice from your vet if you see any of the above signs in your dog. Many of these symptoms may be indicative of other illnesses. Your vet will be able to investigate the problem and provide appropriate advice and treatment.

Worming Products

There are a wide variety of worming products available from a number of different sources. These products vary in activity spectrum (the worms they treat or prevent), how you administer the treatment (spot-on / injection / oral medication), dosage instructions and speed or duration of activity. Always check with your vet before initiating a worming regime. This way you can be confident that you are using the most appropriate products, and following the best treatment for the needs of your dog and family.

How Often Should You Worm?

All animals are at risk from acquiring worm infections. However some animals will be at higher risk than others depending on factors such as their lifestyle and area in which you live. Children are at increased risk of disease from worms; if you have a young family or your dog often comes into contact with children, you should pay particular attention to regular worming. Again, always consult with your vet with regard to the most appropriate treatment schedule.

Control Check List

As well as following a worming plan following consultation with your vet, there are also many other practical things you can do to help prevent the spread of worm infections among your pets and family. These are as follows:

- **'Poop scooping' - make sure you pick up your dog's faeces immediately on a walk and remove it from the lawn or surrounding outdoor environment daily - bag it, and put it in designated poop bins, double bag it, and put it in with the domestic waste, or check with you local council.**
- **Ensure you and your children wash your hands after handling / stroking your dog.**
- **Wash all food including fruit and vegetables before eating them.**
- **Don't allow children to put dirt in their mouths.**
- **Throw away any food dropped on the floor / ground rather than eating it.**
- **Cover children's sandpits when not in use.**

Travelling Pets

There are specific parasitic worms to which your pet may be exposed to on visiting countries outside the UK. Two notable worms are Heartworm (*Dirofilaria immitis*), transmitted by a mosquito bite, which could be fatal if your dog is not protected, and one type of Tapeworm (*Echinococcus multilocularis*), which can cause serious and fatal disease in people.

If you are intending to travel with your dog, you should talk to your vet in plenty of time to establish the best worming regime to ensure the protection of both your dog's health and that of your family. For further information about what you need to do before, during, and after travel abroad with your dog, refer to the Pet Travel Scheme guidelines on the DEFRA website, www.defra.gov.uk/wildlife-pets/pets/travel.

Further reading and information
ESCCAP UK provides practical advice to dog owners to protect pets from parasitic infections and to minimise the risk of their transmission between animals and humans. To find out more, visit www.esccapuk.org.uk.

VACCINATION ADVICE

There are a number of common infectious diseases that dogs are susceptible to throughout their life. Some of these diseases are life threatening and young puppies are particularly vulnerable, so It is important that your puppy is vaccinated against them. Further vaccination as adult dogs may be required to ensure that your dog continues to be healthy and happy throughout its entire life.

Some vaccination may have been carried out prior to you receiving your puppy and a record of this is provided below. Please take this with you on your puppy's first visit to a veterinary surgeon.

Vaccination Given	Age of Puppy	Date Administered
1st	**approx 9 weeks**	
2nd		
Next Vaccination Due:	**see your vaccination card in your pack for further details**	
Please seek the advice of your puppy's veterinary surgeon for information on		

future vaccination. However we strongly recommend you do not do a re-start, so please contact our vet for help if you are concerned,

First vaccinations

Normally, your puppy can receive its first vaccination from approximately eight weeks of age although this can vary depending on the normal practice of the treating vet. The vet will most likely start your puppy on a course of vaccinations against the four main canine distemper, hepatitis, parvovirus and leptospirosis. All of these diseases can be fatal, so after its first course of vaccinations, your puppy may need booster vaccinations according to your vet's advice.

Keeping a record

Once a puppy is vaccinated, the vet will issue a vaccination certificate showing a record of exactly when the puppy was vaccinated and which product was used. This should be kept safe, as you may need to show them at boarding kennels, dog-training classes, or if you take your dog abroad. If you change vet, they may recommend a slightly different regime, and it will be useful to see what vaccination your puppy has had in the past.

Vaccination and socialisation

Until your puppy is fully vaccinated you should prevent them from being exposed to dogs that could be infected or areas that infected dogs could have had access to. Puppies are most receptive to new environments and situations at this age, so keeping them confined to your house and garden may be counterproductive. During these important first weeks at home, you could take your puppy out to different places in your arms or the car to get them used to different situations and noises, as well as letting them meet new people. Further details on socialisation is available in the Kennel Club "Puppy Plan" which can be viewed at www.thepuppyplan.com.

Disclaimer

This guide is to help with your new Bonaforte puppy on a day-to-day basis. The contents are my experiences and they are my opinions.

As an owner, responsibility for the welfare of your hound is yours. Never hesitate to seek expert veterinary care, for sometimes Wolfhounds need to see a vet sooner rather than leaving a condition to see if it improves.

copywright

Printed in Great Britain
by Amazon

58592290R00083